NEW YORK'S 50 BEST

——

Places to take children!

ALLAN ISHAC

ILLUSTRATIONS BY
KATHERINE SCHULTZ

UNIVERSE
New York

Acknowledgments

I'm lucky. Lots of people helped me complete this book: the many parents who spoke with me about great places to visit; my diligent fact-checker, Daniela Echeverria; the brainy folks at Universe Publishing who turned my roughly typed prose into perfect pages just like magic; and finally Unni Benedicte, my friend, who believed in me through two editions of this book, who still thinks my goofiness is a gift, and who looks at me with that sweet smile that tells me everything is okay. You are such a gentle Viking.

First Universe edition published in 2003
by UNIVERSE PUBLISHING
A Division of Rizzoli International Publications, Inc.
300 Park Avenue South
New York, NY 10010

Cover Design: Paul Kepple and Jude Buffum @ Headcase Design
Cover Illustration by Mary Lynn Blasutta
Interior Design by Heather Zschock
Interior Illustration by Katherine Schultz

2003 2004 2005 2006 2007 / 10 9 8 7 6 5 4 3 2 1
Second Edition
Printed in the United States
Library of Congress Catalog Control Number: 2002111512
ISBN: 0-7893-0836-3

Publisher's Note

Neither Universe nor the author has any interest, financial or personal, in the locations listed in this book. No fees were paid or services rendered in exchange for inclusion in these pages. Please also note that while every effort was made to ensure accuracy at the time of publication, it is always best to call ahead to confirm that the information is still up-to-date. All area codes are 212 unless otherwise noted.

To my nieces and nephews,
Amanda, Sarah, Zachary, Alex, and Max,
who have always reminded me to drop
my worries and make balloon animals.
And to Elfie, who has been there
from the beginning.

Contents

16 MORE GREAT PLACES TO TAKE KIDS...Just For the Fun of It!

Introduction

One of the things I love to do when I'm not busy writing books is make balloon animals. I always carry a fistful of balloons in my pocket in case I run into a young friend who would be thrilled to have a bubble mouse or a rubbery sword.

After many years, I've come to recognize a pattern whenever I twist a balloon for a boy or girl with adults standing nearby. The moment I finish the sculpture and hand it to the child, a parent inevitably remarks, "What do you say?" prompting a polite and reflexive "Thank you." What parents don't recognize is that I've already been thanked by the child's simple smile and delighted eyes. Those expressions of gratitude say so much more than words.

I relate this story for a reason — to make the point that I did not pick the places in this book, children did. Not by the things they said (which are often unreliable because kids are trying to please hovering parents), but by their reactions. These can be trusted, and children have responded to the locations in this book with dazzling smiles, wide eyes, infectious laughter, and boundless enthusiasm.

I have not listed hours of operation for any of the fifty places in this book because opening and closing times change often. Always call ahead or check Web sites for up-to-the-minute information and a schedule of special events for your children. In addition, you'll find a note on the **Ideal Age Group**, which is based on my observations of children visiting the fifty locations. These are suggested ages, which will vary, just as children do. Ultimately, you must be the final judge of whether a particular place is appropriate for your child. I know that many parents peruse books like this one for new and unique birthday party ideas, too. Most of the locations in this book can accommodate your birthday group, so call in advance for details.

Every location description ends with a **Cool Kid's Corner.** This is my special note written specifically for children, and I ask that you read it to your child if he or she is unable to do so. This is my small way of connecting directly with the kids.

Finally, I must thank all the parents, grandparents and teachers who have purchased this book, recommended it to friends, and contacted me with suggestions of their own. I'm honored that you've enjoyed the book. I've gotten a lot of joy from sending children to places where they can play, have fun and go on great adventures. Now it's up to us, the parents, the aunts and uncles, the godmothers and grandfathers, to be admiring adults — to give our children as much loving praise, attention and approving words as possible. That's all they need to become wonderful, happy, successful grown-ups.

Okay, now let's go have some fun.

Abracadabra

Address: 19 West 21st Street, between
Fifth and Sixth Avenues • Phone: 627-5194
Ideal Age Group: 5 to 12 • Admission: Free to browse

How big are your eyeballs? They'd better be very big, because at Abracadabra there's so much to see your eyes won't get a minute's rest.

This enormous gag, gift and gadget shop is truly one of most fantastic visual experiences on the planet. Doubt me? Here's a short list of startling stuff you'll see before you've stepped three feet inside Abracadabra's front door: a towering stuffed polar bear, a hilarious fun-house mirror, glittering Mardi Gras masks, giant gargoyles looming over the balcony, rows of delicate porcelain dolls, a live, screeching macaw flying inches above your head, several severed arms, an eight-foot blue Ice Queen, pairs of feathery angel's wings dangling from the ceiling, a wax-like Hulk Hogan in lunge position, and a display case stocked with gruesome alien babies in jars.

It's obvious that owner Paul Blum likes to collect wacky stuff, and every oddball prop, amusing costume and massive stuffed animal here is for sale or rent. In fact, the prop managers at *Saturday Night Live* and *Late Night with Conan O'Brien* are regular clients because, well, where else are you going to find a seven-foot tall, blood-stained Abominable Snowman for your show's Himalayan skit?

Abracadabra is known as the Halloween capital of the city and the title is well earned. They keep more than 20,000 costumes in stock from life-like gorilla suits and oversized rabbit getups to ornate gladiator armor and 1950's drum majorette uniforms. Maybe a major Hollywood film studio has a costume inventory this extensive, but I doubt it. Abracadabra is also the mecca for professional theatrical makeup (I loved the ghoulish scars and oozing wounds), plus wigs in every style and color, a huge collection of dramatic boa scarves, and the most hilarious assortment of rotting yellow hillbilly teeth I've even seen.

Paul is especially fond of horror props so there is merchandise here that can spook your littlest kids (mummies, skeletons, the bloodied woman hanging from a noose, a caged nine-foot crocodile with ferocious teeth that appears ready to chomp), but there are also plenty of friendly toys, puppets, cowboy hats, and other harmless gags to distract your five-year-old from any nearby decapitations in progress. Of course, when the average nine-year-old boy sees the snotty nose gag or the collection of awesome samurai swords, he'll think he went to heaven.

COOL KID'S CORNER: I know what you're thinking ... with a name like Abracadabra, where's the magic? It's right here every Saturday (2 P.M. and 5 P.M.) and Sunday (1 P.M. and 3 P.M.) on their spectacular, red-curtained stage. New York's finest magicians come out to perform an hour-long magic show especially for children ... and it's always FREE for you and me!

Alice in Wonderland Sculpture

Address: Central Park near Fifth Avenue and 74th Street
Ideal Age Group: 2 to 7 • Admission: Free

If you've accepted popular arguments about computers and television and our high-speed technoculture affecting a child's ability to enjoy the slower, simpler pleasures of life, let me present the Alice in Wonderland Sculpture.

There are no bells or whistles here, no keyboards to click, no flashing lights, no microprocessors, not a flicker of fast-paced movement anywhere. It's about as low-tech as you can get. Yet, every day, children exit the information highway to make an enthusiastic pit stop at this delightful sculpture — a virtual city landmark that's been drawing kids like a big bronze magnet for nearly forty years.

To be perfectly honest, I never much liked Lewis Carroll's *Alice in Wonderland* story as a child — too convoluted and weird. But you don't have to appreciate the book to enjoy this sun-swept, south-facing sculpture. Just one glimpse at the ten-foot-tall Alice astride her giant toadstool — surrounded by the whimsical characters from the story — and every fiber of a child's body shouts "Climb!" I've even seen two-year-olds bound out of their strollers to explore the underworld of Alice's mushroom forest.

Sculpted by Jose DeCreeft, this memorial was a gift from

philanthropist George Delacorte to his wife, Margarita, who according to the dedication inscription, "loved all children." If there's any question that all children love her sculpture, just examine handholds like the Cheshire Cat's ears, the mouse's tail, the rabbit's pocket watch, and Alice's extended right arm — all burnished to a bright bronze shine by the sweat and oil from thousands of eager little hands.

I must confess, the temptation to climb into Alice's broad lap and rest my head against her shoulder overcame me. A few five-year-olds stared and wondered why — but Alice didn't seem to care.

A cautionary note to parents: A favorite challenge for children older than eight seems to be a fast ascent to the top of Alice's head, where they hold on to her hair bows like reins. This looks unnecessarily risky to me, especially since the sculpture's base lacks that "soft fall" rubbery surface appearing in so many outdoor playgrounds these days. I'd keep an eye on kids of all ages.

COOL KID'S CORNER: Here's a fun game for children under six: see if you can find the lizard under the big toadstool, the caterpillar on the old tree, the squirrel popping out of his tree hole, the little snail, and the Style 10/6 card in the Mad Hatter's top hat.

American Museum of Natural History

Address: Central Park West at 79th Street
Phone: 769-5100 • Ideal Age Group: 4 to 12
Admission: $10 adults/$6 children (suggested)

Environmentalist Rachel Carson once wrote, "And then there is the world of little things seen all too seldom. Children, perhaps because they themselves are smaller and closer to the ground than we, notice and delight in the small and inconspicuous."

It is precisely this wonderful quality about children that makes visiting the American Museum of Natural History with them such a pleasure. You're pointing out the tall, lethal-looking horns on a herd of gemsbok, while your five-year-old is staring at a hidden snake in the grass. You're fixated on the rippled muscles of the big leopard, while your child wants to know if the little black pig is going to be eaten. It happens every time — just when you think you're going to wow them with the big attraction, kids catch a subtlety that breathes new life into a diorama you've seen fifty times. Through a child's eyes, you get to see all the little stuff, the details you might never have noticed walking through this mammoth museum alone.

This isn't to say kids won't love the really BIG exhibits.

In fact, it's the towering Barosaurus and the dagger-jawed T-rex, along with the rest of the crowd-pleasing dinosaurs that totally thrill and astonish children. If these fearsome fossils look colossal to you, just imagine how they look from three feet below you. One reminder though: the immensely popular Fossil Halls will bring you and the kids back again and again, but other families have caught Jurassic fever, too. Get here early, just after the bony beasts have had breakfast, and your visit will go much easier.

Although every dimly lit corner of these hallowed halls can seem slightly scary to smaller children, you'll need little coaxing to get the kids enthused about the giant Olmec Head with the pudgy face, those determined Haida Indians, still paddling their dugout war canoe after all these years, and the moon rocks (definitely not Swiss cheese) in the Meteorite Hall.

The dance costumes in the African Peoples Exhibition are also sure to elicit oohs and ahhs — look for Yahveh, a marvelous costume that's a cross between Chewbacca, the Midas Muffler Man, and a broom. From fall to early spring, children must see the tropical Butterfly Conservatory — a steamy vivarium where literally hundreds of the brightly colored insects flutter around your head and perch on your shoulder to rest awhile.

COOL KID'S CORNER: There's no question that Tyrannosaurus rex and other reptilian earth shakers were ferocious predators. For proof, just take a look at the Allosaurus fossil in the Hall of Saurischian Dinosaurs. You'll see its bones deeply clawed during a savage fight. The horned Triceratops also shows evidence of a massive wound, this one a crushing blow to the left side of its skull. Ouch, I think that Stegosaurus just hit me.

Asphalt Green AquaCenter

Address: 555 East 90th Street at East End Avenue
Phone: 369-8890 • Ideal Age Group: 2 to 12
Admission: $20 adults/$8 kids for drop-in swim

One of my fondest memories of childhood is splashing around with my friends at the community swim club. It was nothing fancy, just a crisp, clean pool with two lap lanes, a diving area, and a shallow end where we played Blind Man's Bluff and dove for pennies until the tips of our fingers turned to white raisins. That pool was cool.

New York City's public pools, on the other hand, have received some bad press in recent years for being generally unclean and unsafe. And because there are so few of these city-managed swimming holes, they are overcrowded, too. What's a little fish to do?

I strongly recommend grabbing the swimsuits and nose plugs and anchoring the family at the best indoor pool in the entire city — the Asphalt Green AquaCenter. This contemporary complex was built from the architecturally significant shell of the former Municipal Asphalt Plant — hence "Asphalt." "Green" refers to a regulation-sized, artificial turf soccer field that forms the emerald core of this handsome sports facility, and is available for free walk-on use.

The large, chlorine-clean aquatics area is a wonderland for water lovers, refreshingly painted in a get-you-in-the-spirit aquamarine blue. Asphalt Green has two magnificent pools — a fifty-meter Olympic-size pool that has been host to major competitions, and an eighteen-by-twenty-six-foot sister pool used for water babies classes and physical rehabilitation. The therapeutic waters of this smaller pool are kept at a toasty 88° F.

Parents are free to watch the family frogs from a dry spectator gallery overlooking the pools, but it's much more fun to get waterlogged with the kids, taking your belly flops and playing those dipping and dunking games. The AquaCenter also has kickboards and pool buoys, along with those brightly colored foam noodles for keeping kids afloat. If your child is a serious water sprite, enroll him or her in the innovative swim school classes geared to every level from doggie paddlers to fearless backstrokers.

After an $8 million renovation in 2001, the adjacent, parabola-shaped Murphy Center is now a complete sports facility with a kid-sized basketball gym, gymnastics rooms, an elevated indoor running track, and more. The Murphy Center also houses the Lenny Suib Puppet Playhouse (see page 103) for exceptional weekend puppet shows in an intimate 100-seat theater.

COOL KID'S CORNER: You won't believe this, but the floor of the Olympic-size pool here is hydraulic, meaning it can move up and down. In a matter of minutes, one end can go from six-feet deep to a shallow three feet. It can even be raised to zero feet. Imagine if you could do that in your bathtub — water would splash all over the floor!

Books of Wonder

Address: 16 West 18th Street bet. Fifth and Sixth Avenues
Phone: 989-3270 • Ideal Age Group: 2 to 7
Admission: Free Sunday story readings at 11:45 A.M.

In his fascinating classic *The Read-Aloud Handbook,* Jim Trelease presents compelling evidence that the practice of reading to children is essential for awakening young imaginations, improving language skills, even bringing families closer together. He goes further to cite a 1980's National Academy of Education study that concluded, "The single most important activity for building the knowledge required for eventual success in reading is reading aloud to children."

The facts are irrefutable — a child who is read to regularly becomes a better reader, and good early readers go on to be enthusiastic students. There's even evidence that prenatal reading has a positive effect on an unborn child's learning abilities! All of which is overshadowed by the simple fact that reading aloud is fun for both adult and child.

My observation is that parents are reading to children like never before. But when you're simply maxed out on picture books, or run low on reading steam, there's help available from a few excellent children's bookstores with regular story hours — some embellished with appearances by lovable storybook characters in costume.

For many years, one dedicated children's bookstore has been a reliable friend to kids who love stories, offering delightful weekly presentations in a clean, pleasant environment—Books of Wonder. The store's consistently friendly, animated readers have access to thousands of titles in this bright, colorful, carpeted store, so your children are always exposed to the best in classic and contemporary picture books.

Parents will also note that Books of Wonder has one of the largest selections of collectible children's books in the city, including all those we loved: The Hardy Boys, Nancy Drew, The Bobbsey Twins, along with early editions of Frank Baum's *The Wonderful Wizard of Oz*.

If Books of Wonder's downtown location is inconvenient, here are some other Manhattan bookstores with regular readings: **Barnes & Noble** (240 East 86th Street at 2nd Avenue/794-1962) and **The Bank Street Bookstore** (610 West 112th Street at Broadway/678-1654). Check with your local library, too. They often have a children's reading nook with a scheduled story hour each week.

COOL KID'S CORNER: Some of your favorite authors and illustrators come to Books of Wonder just to see you. Ask for a calendar of appearances by best-selling children's writers like J.K. Rowling (the *Harry Potter* series), Chris Van Allsburg (*The Polar Express, Jumanji*), Eric Carle (*The Very Hungry Caterpillar*), and Hillary Knight (illustrator of the *Eloise* stories).

Bronx Zoo

Address: Bronx River Parkway at Fordham Road, Bronx
Phone: 718-367-1010 • Ideal Age Group: 4 to 12
Admission: $11 adults/$6 children
Web site: www.wcs.org

Even if there were nothing here but the apes — Pattycake, Timmy, and the rest of the gorilla gang scrambling for vegetables and mugging for photos — this wonderful zoo would still be a surefire favorite, the no-brainer of unbeatable places to take children.

As it turns out, the largest urban zoo in the country has room for 4,000 other animals, all humanely kept in spectacularly designed natural habitats within the park's 265 acres. Now, with the addition of the new Congo Gorilla Forest, it's possible for you and your children to go on an African safari to see lions and the big silverback gorillas one minute and trek through the bat-infested jungles of Asia the next.

The famous reptile house, where I got my first look at a steely-eyed crocodile as a kid, still has the kind of slithery attractions that children never forget — like Samantha, a twenty-five-foot python and the largest snake on exhibit in the country (with a torso twice the size of my thigh). If you're raising a young zoologist with a fondness for monkeys, walk over to JungleWorld, a rainforest-like setting that's home to playful gibbons, as well as a pair of intense black panthers. And pray that your noggin doesn't look like a ripe mango, because broad-winged fruit bats dart just inches above your head.

The Bengali Express, a guided monorail tour that passes over Wild Asia, offers a close-up look at young rhinos and rare sika deer. During my last visit the line for this ride was long, but once I was on the open-sided cars, close encounters with powerful elephants and regal Siberian tigers made the wait seem worthwhile.

If you're escorting children under seven, make tracks to the Children's Zoo (separate fee of $2 for adults and kids). This smaller enclosure within the wildlife park has short, mulch-lined walkways that are gentler on a child's easily fatigued legs. The general theme at this mini-zoo is "do as the animals do." So when I go, I make myself very small to squeeze through the prairie dog tunnels in a dirt mound adjacent to the real thing (fun, but best left to tinier bodies). Then I take the leap test to see if I can jump farther than a bullfrog (the frog always wins), or I crawl inside one of three human-sized turtle shells. Finally, I like to stop by the petting zoo, buy a handful of food pellets that look like Grape Nuts and let a brown llama tickle my palm with a soft muzzle. The adorable hip-high miniature horse, however, always wins my heart.

COOL KID'S CORNER: Ever wonder what it would feel like to be a lizard escaping down a hollow tree? You can find out at the Children's Zoo where they've placed a slippery spiral slide inside a giant imitation oak. Just climb the stairs to the tree house and take the long ride down. After four topsy-turvy descents during a recent visit, my girlfriend said we had to go. Darn, the other kids got to stay!

Central Park Wildlife Center

Address: 830 Fifth Avenue at 64th Street
Phone: 861-6030 • Ideal Age Group: 2 to 12
Admission: $3.50 adults/50¢ children
Web site: www.centralparkzoo.org

I had just picked my spot around the open-air pool to watch the 4 P.M. sea lion feeding. The sleek brown swimmers were doing that neck-craning thing they do — hoisting themselves up on the rim of their glass-enclosed sea, snorting a fine spray, trying to catch a glimpse of the fish-filled buckets coming their way. Nearby, an excited little boy with his nose pressed against the tank said to his friend, "Tommy, when you grow up do you want to work at the zoo?"

Putting aside any personal feelings you have about small urban zoos caging wild animals, you can appreciate just how magical the Central Park Wildlife Center must be to a four-year-old who would ask this question. To him, the zoo is so cool, so captivating, so much fun, he'd like to spend the rest of his life here. That's a major endorsement. Time to book the play date.

Even if you live in the city and have visited the Wildlife Center a hundred times, make it a hundred and one — there's always more for you and your kids to discover here. I never saw the red pandas napping in the trees until my fourth trip, and I often find peculiar new critters in the Rainforest who were hiding on previous visits. Don't forget, too, that kids thrive on the repeat experience, which gives them a sense of mastery over their environment. I love to watch children confidently escorting smaller siblings along the richly land-scaped paths to see the "ice bears" or the monkeys with the "red tushies." This zoo is particularly well-suited to tiny bodies with little feet, because they can meander easily through the entire compact habitat in a short time.

First, stop in the Rainforest, where you'll find hundreds of monkeys (the white-maned tamarins will charm you), reptiles, and tropical birds, along with tanks of exotic fish (turns out piranhas really can strip the flesh off a city rat in seconds). This steamy, two-story natural jungle — an ideal antidote for cold winter days — also houses a humongous ant farm where children can watch thousands of leaf-cutter ants dart through deep catacombs via miniature closed-circuit camera.

From here, children usually lead the way to favorite destinations like the polar bear exhibit where Gus, the internationally known brooder, has all but stopped his compulsive swimming laps. I also like the shivery Edge of the Ice Pack because I can't get enough of those zippy penguins shooting out of the water bolt upright onto the rocky shoreline.

COOL KID'S CORNER: Before you leave the neighborhood, stop by the zoo's north gate below the Delacorte Clock. Every half hour the time is chimed while you watch the slow pirouettes of an elephant on accordion, a hippo playing the violin, a mountain goat tooting a flute, a penguin beating a drum, a dancing bear with a tambourine, and a horn blowing Mama kangaroo with her baby. And, of course, there's the playful pair of monkeys on top thumping the bell!

Chelsea Piers Sports & Entertainment Complex

Address: Piers 59 to 62 at 23rd Street on the Hudson River
Phone: 336-6666 • Ideal Age Group: 2 to 12
Admission: Free to piers/Activities as low as
$5.00 for all-day roller rink access
Web site: www.chelseapiers.com

This gigantic waterfront sports and recreation center was built on the kind of scale New Yorker's love — what I call "the only" scale. Chelsea Piers is the only four-story, year-round golf driving range in the country, the only indoor ice skating rinks in Manhattan (one each for hockey and figure skating), the only outdoor, professionally surfaced roller-blading rinks in Manhattan (with a new Extreme Park), and the only gymnastics training area in New York City sanctioned for competition by USA Gymnastics. And that doesn't even cover the largest and longest categories – largest rock climbing wall in the Northeast and world's longest indoor running track, at a quarter mile.

Those of us familiar with the imposing size of skyscrapers might best comprehend the sheer mass of this complex by thinking of four eighty-story buildings lying down. Stretched over historic shipping piers, all 1.7 million square feet are designed to deliver peak, high-energy fun for sports-starved children and adults.

The central attraction for kids is the main Field House, which includes two indoor AstroTurf soccer fields, a twenty-eight-foot rock climbing wall designed especially for children, basketball courts, four batting cages ($1 for ten swings), and a massive gymnastics facility (in-ground trampoline, rings, pommel horses, balance beams, parallel bars, you name it). Be sure to take a plunge into the foam-filled diving pit, too, but hang on to your keys.

The Sky Rink was more or less the catalyst for Chelsea Piers. Developer Roland Betts was looking for a practice facility for his figure skating daughter, Jessie, after the original Sky Rink closed on 33rd Street. Good father that he was, Betts got some friends together, borrowed $130 million, and erected this mega sports mall. Now Jessie and every other kid in New York can turn figure eights twenty-two hours a day.

I've never been to an Olympic Sports Village, but it must be a lot like this — safe, sanitized, steeped in primary colors, with athletes of every age, from around the world, walking in leotards and Lycra, looking fit and healthy. The user-friendly Chelsea Piers is such a total sports resource, a growing number of area schools are abandoning their physical education programs and bussing their kids over here to have an absolute field day.

COOL KID'S CORNER: I don't know many kids who are golfers (on the other hand, Tiger Woods must have started young), but whether you own golf clubs or not, drag your duffer Dad over to the four floors of ball-whacking wildness at the Chelsea Piers Golf Club. You won't believe your eyes when those little white balls are teed up for you automatically. They're retrieved from the 200-yard driving range by machine, too!

Children's Museum of the Arts

Address: 182 Lafayette Street bet. Broome and Grand Sts.
Phone: 274-0986 • Ideal Age Group: 2 to 10
Admission: $5 per person • Web site: www.cmany.org

When I saw the life-sized zebra on the sidewalk I knew I had found the Children's Museum of the Arts (CMA), but I didn't really arrive until a giddy three-year-old handed me a heaping cup of yellow flubber. So much for my note taking — within minutes I was sitting next to my pint-sized friend at a busy art table creating a crude sculpture out of the cold, slippery stuff.

That's what they do best at this informal, vibrant space in SoHo — they bring out the spontaneous creative spirit that thrives inside every child. CMA is the city's only hands-on art museum for children, which means your kids will have a chance to explore tons of multi-sensory activities. Drop-in visitors can explore various messy mediums during daily art projects — including paint, pastels, collage, sand painting, clay sculpture, origami, and more — always under the watchful eyes of at least three adult facilitators, most trained artists themselves.

This special environment is guaranteed to stimulate your child's senses with two floors of arts and crafts tables, mini-performance areas, reading nooks, and interactive exhibitions that immerse kids in exuberant creation.

Little kids don't know much about formal art, but they

know if you stick a few jars of tempera paints in front of them with permission to smear the colorful contents all over a tabletop, it's going to be a blast. Here, children are encouraged to be expressive, independent, playful, and inquisitive as they experiment with artwork — which basically means "anything goes." In fact, the unofficial motto of CMA is: **You can smell it, touch it, and play with it, just don't eat it.**

Downstairs children often swarm to a fantastic play corral called the Ball Pond. Surrounded by a soothing blue mural of underwater images, girls and boys get bouncy, throwing their bodies with obvious pleasure into dozens of huge blue, green, and orange rubber balls. This is ideal for working large muscles and helping kids blow off steam before sitting down to a focused art project. And if your child loves to sing-a-long and make loud music with clanging pans, kooky kazoos, and cheechy maracas, there's a half-hour merry Music Circle every Wednesday through Friday at 3:00 P.M.

I also want to tell you about the giant blackboard table for nonstop chalk art, the two-story art house that's a playroom in the clouds, the cool computers for interactive games, and the twelve-foot dragon made of coffee cans … but I'm out of space. So just go to CMA and make art!

COOL KID'S CORNER: Flubber is fun and you can make it at home with this simple recipe: Put 10 drops of food coloring into a cup of hot water. Add one cup of School Glue. Dissolve two tablespoons of 20 Mule Team Borax into a separate 1/3 cup of water. Pour the Borax solution into the glue/water mixture and STIR IMMEDIATELY. Let sit for 2–4 hours and that's it — you've just made safe, nontoxic flubber!

Claremont Riding Academy

Address: 175 West 89th Street at Amsterdam Avenue
Phone: 724-5100 • Ideal Age Group: 6 to 12
Admission: $60 for 30-minute private lesson;
$50 for 1-hour group class

I wrote a children's video about a youth rodeo in Pennsylvania, and got a chance to see lots of kids competing on horseback. Here were boys and girls small enough to crawl inside a ten-gallon hat — some as young as five — skillfully riding the spirited, full-grown quarter horses. What impressed me most was the level of mastery and poise these children displayed with their mounts — a confidence that would help them in every aspect of their lives.

Lucky for city kids, there is an extraordinary place in the middle of New York City where young people can learn to handle horses with the proficiency of their country counterparts — Claremont Riding Academy. The century-old, five-story stable on 89th Street looks so startlingly out of place tucked into the urban sprawl of the Upper West Side, a visit even for non-riding children should be placed on your must-do list.

If you have children older than six who've caught the riding bug, Claremont — with its fifteen professional riding instructors who respect kids and always stress safety awareness — is an ideal school for equestrian training. The academy offers reasonably priced private lessons (English saddle only) for beginners, as well as after-school and weekend group classes. They also have an acclaimed riding program for handicapped and special needs children (hanging out with horses, it seems, can be very therapeutic). In the summer, Claremont's popular day camp offers kids more concentrated instruction.

Built in 1892 (with few visible improvements since then) the landmark New York City stable is funky but fun, with the horsey essence of hay and manure filling a small ground-floor riding arena open for year-round classes. Claremont boards more than fifty horses here, from ponies and palominos to bays and grays, fully trained for all levels of rider. Whether your child saddles up on Mahoney, Trigger, Wotan, Casco, Tonka, or any of the other well-behaved horses, they'll learn good horsemanship and quickly conquer their fear of big animals. And when your kids become crackerjack horsemen, they can trot through Central Park over more than six miles of picturesque bridle paths.

COOL KID'S CORNER: Know what they have on the floors above the horse stalls? Really old carriages, buggies, and sleds from the days when people traveled the city by horse. And, hey (I know, hay is for horses), see if you can find the two horseshoes embedded in the sidewalk right out front of Claremont. Wonder if a dopey horse stepped in wet concrete a hundred years ago and lost his shoes?

Conservatory Garden

Address: 105th Street and Fifth Avenue
Phone: 860-1382 • Ideal Age Group: 3 to 12
Admission: Free

There are 26,000 acres of parks and more than 860 playgrounds in New York City, but only one formal garden — the spectacular Conservatory Garden on upper Fifth Avenue. Why, you ask, would my child be interested in six acres of precisely planted flower beds, arbor-covered walkways, a perfectly manicured lawn, and two sculpted fountains, without a seesaw or slide in sight? Think fantasy, dear parent, think *The Secret Garden.*

Set off from the rest of Central Park by a mighty wrought-iron fence and sitting below street level, the Conservatory Garden has a stately Victorian presence, a magical not-in-New-York quality that appeals to children. Little girls love to imagine they're stepping through the grounds of an English palace — what better place to play a princess in the court of kings? This has also become a popular destination for bride watching (wedding parties are here every weekend in the spring and summer, using the garden as a bucolic backdrop for photographs), where young misses can pick up style tips for dressing Wedding Bell Barbie.

The carefree safety of the garden also encourages city boys to be more like country kids, darting through countless hidden niches and winding paths, all ideal for a pretend skirmish in Sherwood Forest or a more contemporary game of hide-and-seek with parents and siblings.

Another unusual offering of the Conservatory Garden is a place to sit quietly with your child, flanked by crab apple trees swaying to gentle breezes.

Andy Rooney, the *60 Minutes* commentator, once wrote that simple walks around the block with his father on summer nights as a child did wonders for him as an adult. Carry a good storybook into this pristine setting on a spring day (when thousands of multicolored tulips are in bloom), set yourself down with your favorite four-year-old on a sweet and shady bench, and you'll make an equally lasting impression on your young charge.

The Urban Park Rangers (1-800-201-PARK) offer an active schedule of outdoor workshops, guided walks, and activities for kids conducted throughout our city parks. Give them a call and get on their mailing list. Also note the close proximity of the Dana Discovery Center (see page 119) just five blocks north, where they have exceptional nature programs for children throughout the year.

COOL KID'S CORNER: If you've read Frances Hodgson Burnett's *The Secret Garden*, go quickly to the south end fountain where a bronze Mary and Dickon are playing mischievously. I also heard some children say they saw elves and fairies stepping on the fountain's lily pads. Oh, look, there they are!

Empire State Building Observatory

Address: 350 Fifth Avenue at 34th Street
Phone: 736-3100 • Ideal Age Group: 5 to 12
Admission: $9 adults/$4 children for observatory;
$17 adults/$10 children for observatory and
NY Skyride combo ticket

Class trip, fifth grade, eighty-sixth floor of the Empire State Building. A couple of friends and I were peering over the edge of the outdoor observation deck, pressing our luck with a uniformed guard standing nearby. Eventually he made us step back, then, as if to stress the awesome destructive power of a building this large, he proceeded to share a fascinating bit of trivia that has stuck in my brain for thirty years: "You know, if you dropped a penny from up here it would imbed itself five inches deep in the sidewalk."

Cool! Of course, I had no idea at the time if this worthless factoid was true. But it flamed the formidable mystique of the world's most famous building, and prompted me to buy one of those cheap, five-inch scale models of the quarter-mile-high skyscraper. That prized memento sat on my desk next to a small bronze replica of the Liberty Bell (Philadelphia class trip, eighth grade) until I left for college.

Sure, lots of cities have cool sky-high buildings. But I

think kids get the ultimate Big Apple kick from the original skyscraper—the famous pencil point where King Kong swatted down rickety biplanes and Tom Hanks got the girl in *Sleepless in Seattle* (sure, I've seen *An Affair to Remember*, but what kid remembers?). I also like the Empire State Building's central location in midtown where children get the most visual bang for the buck, picking out notable sights at every compass point and identifying the five states visible from here—let me see, New Jersey, Pennsylvania, Connecticut, Massachusetts and, uhhh … New York!

Kids also enjoy the offbeat adventure of simply reaching the observatory. There are seventy-three elevators in this building, but for some strange reason not one of them goes directly to the eighty-sixth floor. You have to take one car to the eightieth floor, trek through office hallways to another shaft, then finish the trip in a second elevator—all of which seems to punctuate the building's enormous size.

Here's a travel tip: this is one of the world's most popular tourist attractions. Show up at the wrong time and the lines will overwhelm you. I suggest an early arrival at 9:30 A.M. or visit at dinner hour, between 5 P.M. and 8 P.M.

COOL KID'S CORNER: Ask your parents nicely to purchase a combination ticket for NY SKYRIDE (Second Floor, 299-4922). Then, sit down, strap in, and hang on for a computer-controlled, big screen thrill ride that takes you over and under the best of our city's sights. Synchronized to the on-screen action, your seat sways, rolls, bounces, and dives for a real, in-your-face New York adventure. In fact, if the ride hadn't been so short—only eight minutes—I would have included it as a top fifty destination.

FAO Schwarz

Address: 767 Fifth Avenue at 58th Street
Phone: 664-9400 • Ideal Age Group: 2 to 12
Admission: Free • Web site: www.fao.com

There is probably no single name in New York more strongly associated with children than FAO Schwarz. This world-famous toy store has been catering to the fantasies and imaginations of kids since 1862. At holiday time more than 50,000 eager children pull equally enchanted parents through the revolving doors of the Fifth Avenue store every day—a tradition that has continued for generations.

I said hello to the real-life toy soldier who greeted me at the front door on a recent visit, then became hypnotized by the endless spinning, flashing, bobbing, and bouncing of the animated Clock Tower. If you never took a step past the rolling blue eyes and chattering red lips of this famous singing timepiece—with its four tiers of chugging trains, blubbery blimps, and teetering toys—you could still keep a three-year-old fully engaged for fifteen minutes (try that with anything less than ice cream).

Of course, there are aisles and aisles of wonderful distractions, delightfully displayed everywhere you look. When Frederick August Otto Schwarz stocked his shelves with simple European dolls and stuffed bears more than 130 years ago, he couldn't have guessed at the magnificent playroom his employees would create a century later in the world's largest toy store (okay, maybe there's a bigger Toys "R" Us somewhere, but no toy store reigns larger in the minds of kids, and none treats children better).

This place is rocking. There are radio-controlled Formula One racers zipping past your feet, Barbie dolls smiling up at you, GI Joes circling around behind you. Star Wars figures invade this toyland, with wind-up toys squirming in every bin. There are more board games, movie-related action figures and video games than all the fourth graders on earth could play with in a year. Electronic and science toys fill one blinking, buzzing display, while another area is stocked floor to ceiling with stuffed animals, including Truffles the Bear and Patrick the Pup—FAO's lovable mascots. And then there are more Barbies! And Toy Story characters! And … well, you get the idea.

I got lost in the lollipop forest at the FAO Scweetz candy area where you'll see the Gummy Bear totem pole, the twelve-foot chocolate soldier, and the world's largest M&M's selection. One last thing: be sure to catch a ride on the giant robot elevator, GO-TO-FLOOR-TWO, with the red-tinted front window that always makes the busy street scene outside look rosey.

COOL KID'S CORNER: Here's why FAO Schwarz is the coolest toy store in the world—*they let any kid play with any toy in the store*. That means you can hug the teddy bears, swing the light sabers, twist the Gumby's, hop on a pogo stick, or play with the puzzles, and you won't get in a lick of trouble. That's the store rule. So sing "Ho" for FAO.

Forbes Magazine Galleries

Address: 62 Fifth Avenue at 12th Street
Phone: 206-5548 • Ideal Age Group: 5 to 12
Admission: Free

Nietzsche said it, but he could very well have been writing about Malcolm Forbes: "In every real man a child is hidden who wants to play."

Forbes, the consummate capitalist and successful publisher, had a great sense of humor, a wonderful capacity to fill himself with life, an adventurous spirit (he loved ballooning), and a penchant for collecting—most notably, Harley-Davidson motorcycles. And if you visit The Forbes Magazine Galleries, you'll discover that he was also into toys.

When you've got pockets as deep as Forbes', you can shop the auctions for goodies at a brisk pace. (Forbes said of his obsession for toy collecting, "Up went my hand, and it's not been often or long lowered since.") In fact, before he left this earthly playground, he'd gathered up 500 rare toy boats and 100,000 toy soldiers—not to mention a number of other priceless items like presidential letters, Abe Lincoln's stovepipe hat, inventor Charles Darrow's original hand-painted Monopoly game board, and twelve of the ornate Faberge Easter Eggs made for the last czars of Russia. And they're all here to see.

Of course, it's the toys that draw kids from all over the world to this mazelike museum space. For young children accustomed to today's touch-it-all museum experience, the dignified Forbes Gallery might prove a bit frustrating—all these toy soldiers and no backyard to play in. But the elaborate scenes behind the display windows are so meticulously presented, the sheer numbers of rusting warships and tiny tin cowboys so striking, children leave deliciously lost in their imaginations.

None of the antique toys on display here were actual playthings from Forbes' early years, but he was able to snap up some amazing toys as a grown-up, including the only *Lusitania* model manufactured by famous toy ship builder Marklin. The doomed ocean liner lies precariously on the floor of a glass-bottomed sea with dozens of submarines hovering above, the telltale pinging of depth soundings filling the air (nautical music and blasts from throaty boat horns complete the mood in all the model boat galleries).

In the rooms dedicated to toy soldiers, someone has spent a very long time setting up marching scenes and mock battles between 12,000 of the more than 100,000 Civil War soldiers, medieval knights, Plains Indians, GIs, and Aztecs contained in the total Forbes' collection. My only gripe is that several of the display windows are too high for tiny eyes—look for one of the footstools scattered nearby.

COOL KID'S CORNER: "When I was sick and lay abed, I had two pillows at my head, and all my toys beside me lay, to keep me happy all the day." Just place your face in the circular window of Robert Louis Stevenson's *Land of Counterpane* and travel to his magical bedroom playland. You'll see.

Hippo Park Playground

Address: Riverside Park at 91st Street
Ideal Age Group: 2 to 7 • Admission: Free

Near the library of the small North Jersey town where I grew up, we had a thumb-sized park with a big green concrete frog poised to leap out the front gate. He was such a sweet frog, so agreeable when hundreds of drooling toddlers climbed on his head and slid down his back, that the playground was fondly and forever christened Froggie Park.

I imagine it is with this same nostalgic fondness that every child who has ever played at Hippo Park will remember this friendly neighborhood playground when they've grown too big for happy hippos. Why hippos? Nobody knows. Maybe because it's a funny name kids love to say. In any case, there they are—seven adult hippos and six baby hippos, all frozen in various stages of wading and wallowing, some bellowing, others belching a spray fountain of water.

Even watching the park's smallest visitors, it's clear that hippos are happening. I saw an eighteen-month-old face-off with a big bull, shout some unintelligible demands at him with broad gestures, slap him on his broad snout, then march away. Like my Froggie, he was tolerant to the end.

One unusual aspect of this very safe park is that it's cooperatively maintained by the Parks Department and an all-volunteer community group called The Playground Project (870-3070). Consisting primarily of local parents, this hardworking group raises funds for upkeep and improvements in the park, employment of two full-time playground attendants year-round (when's the last time you saw that?), and installation of Riverside Park's first yellow emergency telephone.

Besides the hippopotami, the oval-shaped, intimate playground is ideally designed for kids under seven, with special Sutcliffe swings for toddlers, plenty of conventional swings, two sandboxes (the clean, asbestos-free sand is replaced several times a year), wooden climbing gyms, and four slides including a neat spiral model—all shaded by magnificent fifty-year-old oaks.

Here is every child's favorite thing to do at the Hippo Park: go to the center cluster of adult hippos, and scream as loud as you want into the big bull's cavernous mouth. Smaller kids can finish off by climbing down his throat and sliding out his belly.

COOL KID'S CORNER: For special fun, run to the big boulder at the south end of the playground. Now look closely and see if you can find the little animals clinging to the rock—three bronze turtles, three frogs, two snakes, the rat eating a snake, a bird, and a tiny mouse. They may be hiding, but they're all there—I promise.

Intrepid Sea-Air-Space Museum

Address: Pier 86 at West 46th Street on the Hudson River
Phone: 245-0072 • Ideal Age Group: 5 to 12
Admission: $13 adults/$6 children
Web site: www.intrepidmuseum.org

"War, what is it good for, absolutely nothing, listen to me . . . " So went the sixties song, but listen to *me*. The Intrepid, a World War II aircraft carrier loaded with hundreds of decommissioned military airplanes and artifacts is maximum fun for the whole family.

The imposing flattop is part of the world's largest naval museum—an amazing sight with a complement of three mothballed ships permanently berthed in New York harbor. This moored monument to America's military might changes all the time, too, with frequent visits from active Navy vessels and crews from around the world (plus the amazing Fleet Week with dozens of guest ships every spring!).

The Intrepid, with a long history of activity in World War II and Vietnam, and as an astronaut recovery vessel, is the crown jewel of the fleet. In the cavernous interior hangars, three football fields long, you can watch some gripping war footage in the Carrier Operations Theatre (but with no seats, kids get antsy), walk in the shadow of stubby-nosed Grumman fighters, and shoehorn your body into the cockpit of an actual fighter jet.

The hangar and upper flight decks are stocked with what seems to be every retired military plane and spacecraft the museum could get its hands on (more than seventy)—and some look like they were rescued only moments before hitting the scrap heap. But young children rarely notice the disrepair or the rust; just keep them moving because there's lots to see.

One of the few places young history buffs can actually talk to a World War II veteran is up on the ship's command bridge, where they've stationed a retired sailor loaded with Intrepid trivia. I heard wonderful tales from a ruddy-faced seaman with an authentic forearm tattoo. And when he's done sharing war stories, this patriot polishes a gaggle of bronze instruments to a glossy spit shine.

You've got your choice of a destroyer (the *Edson*) and a missile submarine (the *Growler*) to see next. My choice would be the USS *Growler*. In this former guided missile sub, children can see the tight quarters where submerged sailors lived for weeks at a time. High points of this guided claustrophobia tour include the stainless steel showers (smaller than a Manhattan studio apartment's), sleeping quarters squeezed alongside the missile bays, and hatch doorways you'll definitely conk your head on unless you're under ten and very nimble.

COOL KID'S CORNER: If you were impressed with the alien spaceships in movie classics like *Star Wars* and *Independence Day*, wait until you see the Lockheed A-12 Blackbird—our planet's highest-flying, fastest aircraft. This coal black monster is a deadly sky streaker that flies at Mach 3—triple the speed of sound!

Jodi's Gym

Address: 244 East 84th Street bet. Second and Third Avenues
Phone: 772-7633 • Ideal Age Group: 2 to 12
Admission: Starts at $500 for 17-week class/
$30 for 1-hour class

The medal-winning performances of our men's and women's gymnastic teams in recent Olympics have created a boon for many kid's gyms in the city. Suddenly, children who have never executed a somersault are dreaming of perfect back flips, and parents are signing up aspiring gymnasts for after-school classes.

As long as the surge in kid's fitness continues, one heralded gymnastics studio will be training kids exactly the way they've been doing it in New York for nearly twenty years—Jodi's Gym. Jodi Rosenwasser-Levine, a former competitive gymnast, may well be the innovator of the tumbling tots phenomenon, and if the popularity of her classes are any indication, the offerings here are arguably the best.

While Jodi's Gym has a number of excellent preschool movement classes for the tiniest tumblers, this is not a drop-in play space. It's a bona fide gymnastics training facility with a staff of teachers certified by U.S.A. Gymnastics. A number of Jodi's students have even advanced to compete on a national level. And although Jodi stresses that maximum results in strength, flexibility, coordination, and balance are achieved over time, it is possible for out-of-town visitors to arrange for a short series of classes or even single visits (apparently, the children of actors, celebrities, and foreign dignitaries frequent this Upper East Side location and Jodi accommodates their erratic schedules). So if you're a tourist with restless kids who have had enough of sight-seeing and want to exercise, consider Jodi's.

The focus here is always on fun, and the creative classes for kids under five are filled with delighted shrieks and giggles as children jump and shake, twist and tumble, reach, rattle and roll—all the body movements that are basic to gymnastics. Even the youngest kids are exposed to simple, well-padded apparatus like slides, doughnut mats, rings, bars, balance beams, balls, and bouncers.

There seems to be two important keys to the longevity of Jodi's Gym. First, talented teachers who like to be with kids. Jodi boasts a student-teacher ratio of six-to-one, but in a class of four-year-olds I observed there were actually nine kids to three staffers. I was impressed with a senior instructor who told stories to engage his class while stretching, like the one about the spider walking down the leg to catch the toes (not one kid spaced out during this entire exercise). The other factor is safety. Jodi's Gym is known as one of the safest gyms in the country, with a negligible accident rate. Good news when your daughter's doing her first cartwheel dismount off the balance beam.

COOL KID'S CORNER: If you're into cool leotards, biketards, and skatetards, you'll find a fully stocked active wear store for boys and girls. You gotta look good flipping through the air!

Kerbs Conservatory Water Sailboats

Address: Central Park at 72nd Street near Fifth Avenue
Phone: 917-796-1382 • Ideal Age Group: 4 to 12
Admission: Sailboat rental $10 per hour
E-mail: sailboatguy@hotmail.com

I t has an old-fashioned, almost Victorian feeling about it that is leisurely and agreeable. Sailing a model boat with a young mariner is the kind of activity perfectly paced for an early spring morning or late summer afternoon. And at the Conservatory Water, they even supply the radio-controlled model yachts.

The oval-shaped boat pond sits in a small valley originally intended to be a formal garden with a glass conservatory. But park designers, Frederick Law Olmstead and Calvert Vaux, ran out of money, so the two-acre basin became a venue for ice-skating and model boat races. In 1929, the pond was rimmed with the low concrete wall you see today, so children can lean over and push their boats into the shallow waters.

If you own a model sailboat, you can use the Conservatory Water for sailing from March through early November after securing a $20 season permit (360-8133).

Rental boats are available from mid-April through early November—look for Ron McKechnie (The Sailboat Guy) and his pushcart concession by the three small steps at water's edge. Generally, two boats are recommended, one for parent and one for child, so you can stage your own informal races.

These model boats have no motors, and the radio controls only move the rudders and sails. Still, with the simple handheld control box, even young children can master operation of these mini-yachts in minutes. The rental boats, with sails no higher than eighteen inches, can also be effective for teaching the basic concepts of sailing to those who've never ventured out on a full-sized Sunfish. Somehow, it's a lot easier to practice tacking maneuvers when you're not worried about getting clocked by the mainsail or tossed overboard.

Parents should note that the Hans Christian Andersen storybook statue on the west side of the Conservatory Water is home to a wonderful summer tradition—Saturday morning storytelling at 11 A.M. (end of June through September, 360-8236). Children will hear myths, fairy tales, and legends from around the world, including engaging stories by the renowned creator of this park program, Diane Wolkstein.

COOL KID'S CORNER: If you want to see some really spectacular model boats with polished wooden hulls and sails as tall as you are, take a peak inside Kerbs Memorial Boathouse (at the Fifth Avenue side of the pond next to the food stand). That's where the privately owned yachts are stored, many ranging in price from $500 to $1500. These prized boats are raced by serious sportsmen on Saturday mornings during the summer months.

Kerlin Learning Center
at Wave Hill

Address: West 249th Street and Independence Avenue, Riverdale, Bronx • Phone: 718-549-3200 • Ideal Age Group: 2 to 8 • Admission: $4 adults/$2 children/Free for children under 6/Everyone free November 15–March 15 Web site: www.wavehill.org

Every Saturday and Sunday, fifty weeks a year, the Family Art Project at Wave Hill gives city kids a chance to smell, feel, touch, even taste an unspoiled bit of nature. As they explore the beautiful gardens, spacious lawns, and peaceful wooded trails of this spectacular twenty-eight-acre oasis, children learn about nature by being in nature—a positive, full-immersion experience that brownstone babies just can't get at the local dog run.

When I wrote my book *New York's 50 Best Places to Find Peace and Quiet*, I included Wave Hill as a spectacular retreat for nature-deprived city folk. But I remember thinking how valuable all this open space would be for overcrowded city kids, especially with Wave Hill's creative programs to connect children to the natural world.

On weekend afternoons from 1 P.M. to 4 P.M., your children are placed in the capable hands of visual artist and naturalist, Noah Baen. Since 1990, Noah has guided kids through Wave Hill's lush landscape pointing out the shapes of leaves, the fragrances of flowers, the buzzing and fluttering of bees, butterflies, and birds. In the winter, when nature seems to sleep, Noah cleverly rolls back a big rock to see what crawls out, or finds life on the end of a tree branch where none seemed to exist a moment before.

Then the kids collect stuff: pinecones, seed pods, dry grasses, flower petals, chipped rocks, red berries, twisted gourds, variegated leaves, and all sorts of other wondrous outdoor bounty. Which, under Noah's watchful eye, is creatively transformed by the children into art: floral collages, ornamental wreaths, handmade paper, natural noisemakers, three-dimensional paintings, traditional corn husk dolls, and harvest headdresses. Much of this inspiring work can be found festooning the walls and hanging from the ceiling of the Kerlin Learning Center, located in Wave Hill's main facility—an impressive stone mansion built in 1843.

Noah is a superb teacher and respectful friend to the children who drop in for his inspiring, sensory workshops. He's not afraid to wear a butterfly wing hat to enhance a story about monarch migration, or a leaf mask to explain the miracle of fall foliage. Best of all, he offers each child his focused attention and enthusiastically admires every creation. That's a special gift.

COOL KID'S CORNER: Noah creates unforgettable seasonal festivals like the one in September called *Buzzarama*. It takes place near the active outdoor honeybee hives at Wave Hill where you'll make a cool bee costume, pick up a pollination wand at the Pollination Information Station, and become a bumblebee living in a giant cardboard hive. There's even a beekeeper who will give you a taste of the yummy honey right off the waxy comb.

Liberty Helicopters

Address: VIP Heliport at 30th Street and 12th Avenue
Phone: 967-6464 • Ideal Age Group: 4 to 12
Admission: Varying tours from $50 to $155 per person
Web site: www.libertyhelicopters.com

When I was seven years old, my mother took my sister and me on a helicopter tour from the top of the old Pan Am building in midtown Manhattan. It made such an impression, I can close my eyes today and still feel the lurching liftoff of my first helicopter ride.

There are a couple helicopter sight-seeing services in New York, but the largest and most experienced organization (fifteen years), with the best tours for your dollar is Liberty Helicopter flying out of the west side VIP Heliport. Their six-passenger, red, white, and blue aircraft are extremely safe; in fact, Liberty has been incident-free since their first flights in 1985—important when your family is aboard.

Liberty is open year-round from 9 A.M. to 9 P.M. (including all holidays), so your kids can get a bird's-eye view of the dazzling skyscrapers anytime of the day, in any season (reservations required for two or more). The skyline by night seems to appeal to adults more than to kids, so try to pick a clear day for your trip. And arrive early so your children can spend some time at the heliport's windows watching the constant stream of helicopters glide onto the riverside tarmac. You can also go outside, walk south around the trailer complex, and stand along the storm fence feeling the propellers buffeting the air as the whirlybirds make their vertical ascents.

I recommend The Big Apple flight package ($101 per person), which covers approximately fourteen miles, or about twenty minutes of total experience from takeoff to touchdown. If that sounds quick, consider that every minute is chock-full of high-flying excitement and unforgettable sights. You'll climb above the Hudson River, stare straight into the eyes of the Big Green Lady, then cruise up the river to the George Washington Bridge, passing midtown's magnificent skyscrapers and looping back to the heliport.

Okay, it's pricey. But if you want my advice, save the $400 you'd pay Magnifico The Magician for birthday party entertainment, and take your son or daughter with three best friends to Liberty Helicopter instead. You'll be awarded Parent of the Year.

COOL KID'S CORNER: If you're the birthday boy or girl, ask for one of the double seats in the cockpit next to the uniformed pilot. You'll get a close-up look as he maneuvers the aircraft with a gazillion buttons and switches, and you'll peer down through your legs out the copter's glass nose. You can really feel the G-forces of the banking curves when you're sitting up front. It's totally awesome!

Liberty Science Center

**Address: Exit 14B NJ Turnpike, Liberty State Park,
Jersey City, New Jersey • Phone: 201-200-1000
Ideal Age Group: 5 to 12 • Admission: $14 adults w/ IMAX
Dome Theater/$12 children w/IMAX Dome Theater
Web site: www.lsc.org**

There's no escaping it, when I was young science stunk. Biology, physics, chemistry, it didn't matter, they all left me sleepy and confused. Recess, on the other hand, was fun. I was totally focused during recess. Which leads me to the conclusion that if you could keep recess going while learning science, you'd have a winning formula.

Fortunately, they've figured all that out at Liberty Science Center (LSC) where their motto is Science = Fun, and where they've packed a hulking steel-and-concrete structure with four floors of unforgettable scientific attractions. The moment I entered the front atrium to see the herky-jerky motions of the mesmerizing Hoberman Sphere (a 700-pound aluminum snowflake that explodes robotically from 4.5 feet to 18 feet in seconds), I knew science would never be the same.

This cavernous space reminds me of a vertical pinball machine, with hundreds of high-scoring, hands-on exhibits forming the bumpers, and kids playing the part of the hyperactive balls. The energy at LSC is intense, and children can be quickly over-stimulated—plan to go slow and not rush through in one visit.

That said, let me take you on a brief tour of my favorite discoveries.

First, there's the Torsional Wave, a seventy-foot spinal column of metal rods that ascends to the ceiling three stories up. A sharp tug on the handle convulses the instrument, and traveling waves can be timed to the top and back. Virtual Hoops (or Virtual Ping-Pong) is next; enter the mini-court, slip on a cyber glove, then challenge a team of hootin' and hollerin' computer-generated players as you drive for the virtual basket (I got stuffed five times).

On the second floor, there was the Bernoulli Bench, where I tossed a beach ball toward an invisible column of blowing air and watched it dance and float in magical suspension. And then there's the Equest environmental exhibit where kids can launch an explosive hot water geyser and explore other natural wonders. But my favorite was the world's largest IMAX Dome Theater hiding under that huge silver-skinned dome at LSC. Spectacular movies are projected inside this overhead vault, filling your entire visual field with 180 degrees of dazzling and dramatic pictures. My senses were flying.

All this and I've yet to mention the four-inch-long hissing Madagascar Cockroaches (go ahead, pick them up), the solar telescope for spotting sun flares, and dozens of remarkable mindbenders and interactive puzzles.

COOL KID'S CORNER: Ready for something creepy? Crawl through the pitch-black, 100-foot maze of the Touch Tunnel, where you have to trust every sense but your eyes to get you through. I wriggled my way slowly along, sweating bullets. Fortunately, everybody gets out alive.

Madame Tussaud's New York

Address: 234 West 42nd Street between 7th and 8th Avenues
Phone: 512-9600 • Ideal Age Group: 6 to 12
Admission: $22 adults/$17 children
Web site: www.madame-tussauds.com

You never know who's real at Madame Tussaud's. I stepped into the elevator at this remarkable wax museum to find a life-like statue of a purple-and-yellow-clad usher standing inside. As I reached out to push a floor key, he suddenly sprang to life ... and scared me silly.

Of course, that's what makes Madame Tussaud's so freaky and fun. Every one of the nearly 200 masterfully crafted wax figures looks so startlingly real, you'll find yourself doing constant double takes—did Regis Philbin just blink; wasn't Wayne Gretzky standing over there just a second ago; did Woody Allen wave to us?

The original Madame Tussaud's in London is perennially the city's most popular tourist attraction, but this marvelous, attention-grabbing $50 million museum on 42nd Street is likely to rival it in appeal. The five-story physical structure alone is spectacular with a glass-enclosed viewing platform suspended over the street, the only outdoor glass elevator in New York, and a giant hand reaching over the rooftop displaying a vertical Madame Tussaud's marquee from its fingertips.

But it's the ornately decorated theme rooms inside, filled with all those uncanny wax portraits of famous actors, world leaders, sports stars, and entertainment icons that will have you instantly hooked. I found posing for photographs with my favorite celebrities and comparing physical attributes completely engrossing. Who knew that Yoko Ono was this short, that Jodie Foster's eyes were so electrifyingly blue, or that Brad Pitt wasn't as good-looking in person (or should I say, in wax)?

And you can be sure that all these famous folks have been captured in precise detail by Madame Tussaud's renowned wax artists. In fact, they take more than 250 measurements and photographs of each celebrity, gathering information about hair texture, skin tone, eye color, even birthmarks and scars, before starting these three-dimensional portraits.

In a room called The Gallery, you'll see dozens of historical figures like Mahatma Gandhi, The Dalai Lama, Princess Diana, Abraham Lincoln, and Nelson Mandela. But, of course, it's the stars of sports and pop culture that so many kids come to see; people like Jon Bon Jovi, The Beatles, Michael Jordan, Elton John, Steven Spielberg, The Spice Girls, Bob Marley, and Britney Spears. And yes, I stared up at Kareem Abdul-Jabbar's impossible height—just like all of the other disbelievers.

COOL KID'S CORNER: Check it out—the wax superstars here have their hair washed, their makeup retouched, and their jewelry polished almost daily. And can you guess what part of their bodies celebrities look at first when they see themselves in wax? The back—because it's the view they seldom get to see!

Madison Square Garden Tour

Address: Seventh Avenue bet. 31st and 33rd Streets
Phone: 465-5800 • Ideal Age Group: 5 to 12
Admission: $15 adults/$12 children
Web site: www.thegarden.com

There is no sports fan like a New York sports fan, and they tend to raise little fanatics. If you've got one running around your house wearing a Knicks, Rangers, or Liberty jersey, he or she is going to flip over this one-hour, behind-the-scenes tour of arguably the world's most famous sports arena.

Even before the tour starts, you're treated to large-screen, DVD loop tapes of New York sports teams in action. But the real fan fun begins when the high-energy tour guides appear in colorful team sweatshirts. First, you'll be whisked through a posh, season ticket holders dining room where you view a short video history of the thirty-year-old Garden (built in 1968, it's New York City's fourth Garden sports complex). Then you're taken upstairs to one of the eighty-nine lavish skyboxes overlooking the arena, containing a dozen cushy seats, a kitchen, a bar, and closed-circuit TVs—all available for the current price of just $400,000 per year. These are primarily, and not surprisingly, owned by large corporations to entertain business guests.

The next stop is where kids go absolutely giddy: they're taken directly inside the Rangers, Knicks, or Liberty locker rooms (which one depends on who has a game that night—you visit the other teams' quarters). Here, young fans see the actual players' lockers, their game uniforms, and the physical therapy tables where players get taped up before big games. This is a dream opportunity to take your photo with your favorite players' game jersey or gargantuan basketball shoes.

One seven-year-old on our tour got to slip his foot into the size seventeen sneaker of a New York Knick superstar. Later, a locker room attendant tossed the same ecstatic little boy an official NHL hockey puck—yes, he got to keep it. Then the tour ends as you descend the stairs of this historic 20,000 seat arena to sit on the Rangers, Knicks, and Liberty home bench, listening to amazing facts about the massive Garden scoreboard and the making of the hockey ice (twenty hours). Our tour guide, an enthusiastic and obsessed New York sports fan, finished up by challenging members of our group to a sports trivia quiz. I didn't get one answer right—the seven-year-old got ten.

COOL KID'S CORNER: Take the last tour of the day if you want to bump into one of your favorite Knicks, Rangers, or Liberty players arriving before a game (the guide said it happens all the time). Also look for the mini-hockey rink woven into the rug of the Rangers locker room so coaches can diagram plays between periods, and the specially built Knicks locker room door that's a whole foot taller than any other doorway in the hall.

Mars 2112

Address: 1633 Broadway at the corner of 51st Street
Phone: 582-2112 • Ideal Age Group: 4 to 12
Admission: Children's meals start at $8.95
Web site: www.mars2112.com

When you're visiting another planet, it's always good to know a few words of the alien language, like "vabanu," which means "hello" in Martian. Practice this with the accompanying three-fingered salute and you'll be ready for the best intergalactic dining experience of your earthly life.

No matter what language you speak or planet you call home, you're always welcome at Mars 2112—one of the most entertaining and thoroughly polished, family-oriented theme restaurants in the solar system. If seeing the 25-foot flying saucer in the sunken plaza entrance doesn't convince you that you're in for an otherworldly adventure, perhaps stepping up to the departure gates in Mars 2112's futuristic lobby will.

Once you're issued a Martin Federation visa, you're escorted onto a B-719 Ether Runner spaceship for the five-minute trip to the Red Planet. This 22-seat shuttle craft is able to transcend the space-time continuum as it travels at warp speed, swaying, pitching, and bumping over Manhattan, past the MIR Space Station, and into a worm-hole that catapults the ship towards Mars (all of which you watch from a really cool viewing port).

You arrive on Mars in the year 2112, where you're greeted by tech support crewmen convincingly dressed in blue-and-silver Star Trek-like uniforms. You exit into the dim red interior of a subterranean crater with steaming lava pools underfoot and continue your extraterrestrial adventure. While you wait for your table (keep an eye on nearby video monitors for your number to pop up), you can visit the Mars Bar where parents can sip assorted mars'tinis and kids can enjoy a variety of non-alcoholic celestial concoctions.

The ultimate kid-pleaser (and time killer) is the Cyberstreet Arcade, located in a red rock cave packed with fifty high-energy video and interactive games. From there you step through a narrow passage called the Rock Fissure into one of the two dining venues: the Crater's Edge, a 175-seat balcony area, or the cavernous Crystal Crater, which seats 325 people and includes a massive view-screen showing Martian landscape footage and scenes from Apollo missions.

Leafing through the *Mars Times* (The Galaxy's Most Widely *Red* Martian Newspaper) you'll find a menu featuring space age dishes like Quasar Quesadillas, Galactic Greek Salad, Supernova Spare Ribs, plus special kid's dishes like Pluto's Pasta and Crater Burgers. While theme restaurants are rarely known for their cuisine, I found the fare here to be better than good … it was out of this world!

COOL KID'S CORNERS: Looking for Martians? They appear daily at Mars 2112, an utterly silent species with snouts and rubbery blue and pink skin. You'll meet Captain Orion, Empress Gloriana, and a Martian baby, too— QT∏ (Cutie Pie to earthlings). If you fall in love and want to take her home, you'll find doll-sized QT∏'s in the gift shop.

NBC Studio Tour and
Today Show Viewing

**Address: 30 Rockefeller Plaza at 49th Street bet. Fifth and
Sixth Avenues • Phone: 664-7174
Ideal Age Group: 7 to 12 (Children under 6 will not be
admitted) • Admission: $17.50 adult/$15 children
Today Show viewing is free • Web site: www.nbc.com**

Whenever my star-struck nieces and nephews visit me in the media capital of the world, the question they always ask is, "Will I see anybody famous?" Predictably, we spend a good portion of each day hunting for celebrities—recent strategies include milling around the Ed Sullivan Theater during Letterman tapings, hanging out in front of the MTV studios on Broadway for *TRL* (page 126), or strolling through celebrity-dense neighborhoods like Madison Avenue and the West Village.

But there are two destinations offering a very high probability of celebrity contact—the NBC Studio tour and the adjacent *Today Show* broadcast. The one-hour-and-ten-minute guided NBC tour takes you behind the scenes at the National Broadcasting Company, and it is especially fascinating for older kids held spellbound by the allure of TV. The tour departs from the NBC Sweet Shop by the main elevators and that's where so many celeb sitings occur. Guests from shows like

Late Night with Conan O'Brien and *Saturday Night Live*, as well as local news personalities, pass through the same halls and often ride the same elevators as tour guests.

Tour highlights include *History Theatre*, which presents NBC's early days in radio. I liked the Slap-and-Crack paddle used during radio sports broadcasts to mimic the sound of a bat hitting a baseball. You'll peek into the studios of *Dateline*, *The NBC Nightly News,* and *Late Night* programs, as well as visit Studio 8H, the legendary home of *Saturday Night Live*. You'll also be taken to a working studio for the NBC "interactive experience," which lets you stage an interview with video images of Conan O'Brien or Jay Leno. One member of the tour is usually selected to do an on-screen weather report—I volunteered and forecast an August snowstorm for New York. Wrong.

If you can shake the kids out of bed early enough, you might also consider joining the crowd scene outside the *Today Show* studio. The live broadcast begins at 7 A.M. (until 10 A.M.) and if you arrive an hour early to get a front row position, you'll not only stand nose-to-nose with Katie Couric, Matt Lauer, and congenial weatherman Al Roker, you may even get to be on TV. Bring a cute baby, a dramatic poster, or some other attention-getter and Al is sure to notice you during one of his brief weather spots.

COOL KID'S CORNER: Here are some fun facts I learned on the studio tour—the NBC mascot is a peacock because the network was the nation's first to broadcast in color. And those three tones you occasionally hear during station identifications are the musical notes G, E, C—the initials for NBC's corporate parent, the General Electric Company.

New Jersey Children's Museum

Address: 599 Valley Health Plaza, Paramus, New Jersey
Phone: 201-262-5151 • Ideal Age Group: 2 to 8
Admission: $8 per person • Web site: www.njcm.com

L ittle kids spend a major part of their playtime pretending to be adults—doing important grown-up jobs, dressing up in big people's uniforms, mimicking the words, gestures, and actions of parents and teachers. It was only a matter of time before someone realized that creating a place specifically made for playacting and pretending would be a hit with kids.

Aha! Look no further than the New Jersey Children's Museum. I know what you're thinking—since when did Paramus become one of the five boroughs? Since I decided that if you can drive out to the suburban malls to shop, your kids can enjoy a fun-filled afternoon as a surgeon, a ballerina, a knight in armor, a fireman, a helicopter pilot, a newscaster, an astronaut, an archaeologist, a construction worker, a boat captain, a postal worker, a chef ... whew, I'll run out of space before this 15,000-square-foot playpen for pretending runs out of ersatz professions!

The museum's converted warehouse location doubles as an exciting learning environment and world of fantasy, where kids are encouraged to touch and try everything. Do you have an aspiring construction worker in the house? The museum has a genuine orange Tiger Excavator in a nifty area that includes building blocks, construction toys, and cut-aways of the warehouse structure itself so children can identify I-beams and cinder blocks.

For future pilots, they've flown in an authentic Hughes 269 helicopter with its dome cockpit and dashboard dials still in place. Your daughter the doctor can perform triage in a new play ambulance with working stethoscopes, surgical gowns, and X-rays hanging from a light box. One of the most popular destinations is a mock grocery store complete with stocked shelves, kid-sized metal pushcarts, and a check-out register.

Of the more than forty permanent exhibits, one of the best was a fully functioning television station, WKIDS, where children can watch themselves doing the news on two TV monitors. Right behind that was a ten-foot-tall Fantasy Castle with formidable turrets, a kids-only velvet throne room, and an assortment of medieval costuming to stage a Renaissance Fair. Over at the horse stable, rodeo kids can ride stuffed stallions, while space travelers can use computer play stations in the 20-foot high rocket ship. And for sheer fun, there's a new waterplay exhibit, where children can control water jets, squirt targets, and blast each other without getting wet!

What do you want to be when you grow up? The New Jersey Children's Museum is the place to find the answers.

COOL KID'S CORNER: Climb aboard the real, 1954 open-cab fire engine that's ready to roll. Turn on the red flashing lights, pull the yellow cord to clang the bell, and rush to a blaze in full fire gear. You drive, I'll pull the pumper hoses. Let's go!

The New Victory Theater

**Address: 209 West 42nd Street bet.
Seventh and Eighth Avenues
Phone: 646-223-3020 • Ideal Age Group: 6 to 12
Admission: Show tickets are $10 to $30
Web site: www.newvictory.org**

They call it "the family treat on 42nd Street" for good reason. New Victory is Manhattan's oldest active theater — an intimate, elegant, 500-seat jewel box built by Oscar Hammerstein in 1900 that has now been lovingly restored as New York City's first performing arts theater exclusively for children and families.

Before 1996, Forty-second Street was the last place on earth you'd want to bring your kids. A fashionable theater district at the turn of the century, it had deteriorated by the 1970s and 1980s into a seedy strip of X-rated movie houses and peep shops. But under the direction of an independent, nonprofit organization called The New 42nd Street Inc. this historic block was revitalized and refurbished, and The New Victory became its first crowning achievement, followed by The New Amsterdam Theater ("The Lion King" venue), Madame Tussaud's (see page 54), and other stellar attractions for kids.

In this ornate, double-balconied auditorium—decorated in deep reds and gold, with eight pairs of chubby cherubs dangling their feet from the rim of a splendid central dome—

young people are treated to a dozen dazzling productions of innovative new shows and celebrated classics every season. And make no mistake—this is not frivolous kiddie theater, unsuitable for adults in tow. These are thoughtful, inspiring, sometimes gritty or amusing stage productions, professionally performed with astonishing sophistication. Suddenly, great theater has been made accessible to kids—in their very own playhouse.

The New Victory has assembled a magical mix of presentations, from the cutting-edge insanity of Australia's "Circus Oz," to acclaimed movement performances by the Parsons and Alvin Ailey dance companies. There have been dramatic plays, Bunraku-style puppetry, fabulous film festivals, and comedy acts, too, including the hilarious juggling and clowning of the Flying Karamazov Brothers—a favorite show that always leaves the audience giggling contagiously. A complete program of the full season schedule is available by calling The New Victory.

If there is any doubt that this handsomely restored theater has thoughtfully considered the entertainment needs of children, I'd like to point out one important detail: the seating is raked more sharply than any I've ever seen. Which means that it's very easy for little heads to see over grandma's big hair.

COOL KID'S CORNER: They rebuilt the Victory's grand exterior staircase so kids like you could race to the top before the show begins. Once inside, look closely at the end of each row of seats. See those carved bumblebees—they were put there long ago by a former Victory owner named David Belasco. Get it ... BEE-lasco.

New York Aquarium

**Address: West 8th Street and Surf Avenue,
Coney Island, Brooklyn
Phone: 718-265-3474 • Ideal Age Group: 5 to 12
Admission: $11 adults/$7 children/under 2 years free
Web site: www.nyaquarium.com**

Sharks can smell prey a mile away, hear prey a half-mile away, see prey fifty feet away, and taste prey as they chomp away! But at the New York Aquarium you can get almost close enough to these ferocious-looking, prehistoric predators to brush those multiple rows of razor sharp teeth.

Although the aquarium celebrated its 105th anniversary in 2001 (the oldest continually operating aquarium in the nation), this waterside home to sharks, stingrays, beluga whales, walruses, dolphins, and thousands of fish and marine mammals is no longer the uninspired tank farm I remember from school outings as a kid.

For one thing, the aquarium now has the feeling of a natural habitat, like the dramatic Sea Cliffs Exhibit, for instance—a 300-foot rocky re-creation of a Pacific coastal habitat for sea otters, penguins, seals, and blubbery 3,000-pound walruses. You can prepare to be splashed at a new 1,600-seat Aquatheater, featuring Sea World-type shows twice a day with the air-and-sea antics of bottlenose dolphins and barking sea lions. Maybe I'm an easy audience, but to me there are few things as exciting as a streaking dolphin flying through the air to pluck a herring from the outstretched lips of his trainer.

Explore The Shore features a Touch Tank filled with live sea stars, horseshoe crabs, and urchins, along with other hands-on marine exhibits. There's also the amazing Crash Cave where you can live out your fantasy of being a barnacle. Every thirty seconds a man-made wave explodes overhead as you experience the unbelievable force of shoreline surf while remaining dry and unscathed. Wow, hang on!

The Shore also houses a crowd-pleaser called "Zap!" Here your children can compare their body's electrical charges to the 650 volts generated by a slithery electric eel. Ugly, ugly, ugly. But the hyperactive, amplified crackles and pops of the measuring devices are cool for kids.

While the aquarium's odd-looking family of beluga whales (including the world's first whale born in captivity) is a perennial favorite, it's hard not to dash off to the 90,000-gallon shark tank the moment you arrive. Standing with your nose inches away from the deadly teeth and beady eyes of circling behemoths like Big Bertha (a 400-pound, 10-foot sandtiger) throws you and the kids into a delirious state of exhilaration and fear.

COOL KID'S CORNER: Could you stand the freezing cold of ocean life? Can you hold your breath as long as a seal? You can answer these and other questions in the Sea Cliffs Exhibit. I held my breath for forty-five seconds (a seal can dive for twenty minutes), and the icy metal plate used to test skin for deep-water cold tolerance made me shiver. I guess I'll stay a human.

New York Doll Hospital

Address: 787 Lexington Avenue bet. 61st and 62nd Streets
Phone: 838-7527 • Ideal Age Group: 5 to 12
Admission: Free

O nly in New York. Actually, this dedicated doll hospital is
the only one in the entire United States. If that isn't reason enough to take the kids, how do 100 upside-down porcelain heads grab you? Or an equal number of spare torsos
hanging from the backroom rafters?

I'm going to tell you right up-front that the New York Doll
Hospital is a mess. Arms here, assorted legs over there, a pile of
wigs in the corner, boxes full of eyeballs in the back. You'll probably be stunned by the chaos and clutter, but any child who's
ever left his toys lying around is going to love this place.

The 100-year-old doll hospital is not only an international institution, it's the last survivor of a fast-dying art. It's
also incredibly weird (and small, too, so they ask you not to
bring school groups). But if you can overlook the monstrous
muddle for a minute, you'll notice something. Broken, bat-
tered, and bruised dolls of every size, shape, and pedigree are
admitted here—and that's because proprietor Irving Chais is
probably the finest doll doctor in the world.

Irving's grandfather started the hospital around 1900,
and it's been in the family ever since. Irving grew up restring-
ing dislocated arms, repairing torn dresses, and re-gluing

pulled out hair. Today, the world's most respected doll manufacturers send him their repairs, and private collectors from as far as South Africa and Australia trust only Irving to treat their valuable Shirley Temples. He still works six days a week saving the lives of treasured dolls, assisted by an equally dedicated doctor from Colombia, a dressmaker who's been with him for thirty-five years, and his daughter who specializes in wig reconstruction.

While he's not doing much surgery anymore, Irving is constantly digging out original spare parts for the vinyl, rubber, tin, wood, plastic, porcelain, papier-mâché, and clay dolls brought here for repair. Besides his encyclopedic knowledge of dolls (he can identify the maker and country of origin of any doll you shove at him in seconds), Irving is also a funny man with some practiced one-liners. He's fond of saying that the hospital has "never lost a patient," and that his medical malpractice costs are zero.

COOL KID'S CORNER: Irving, who likes to play the grumpy old man, really adores kids and will be thrilled to show you his kooky collection of body parts. Ask him to take you in back to see the hundreds of pairs of glass eyes, and the big box of creepy doll teeth. You're gonna love this guy.

New York Hall of Science

Address: 47-01 111th Street,
Flushing Meadows Corona Park, Queens
Phone: 718-699-0005 • Ideal Age Group: 5 to 12
Admission: $7.50 adults/$5 children
Web site: www.nyhallsci.org

The good news is they've packed so many gee-whiz thrills into the spellbinding exhibits at the New York Hall of Science, your kids will devour every soft scientific principle with glee. The bad news is, not a child on earth could happily transition to a school textbook after a day on this unforgettable field trip. Oh well, sound bite science is fun.

There are more than 225 amazingly cool, interactive exhibits here that look nothing like the boring, brain-drain experiments of my youth. In fact, I liked this hands-on science museum so much, I couldn't keep my hands off. I went back three times in one month.

The Hall was originally built as a pavilion for the 1964–65 World's Fair and they still have some circa aerospace artifacts rusting outside. But don't let these relics fool you—there's cutting edge intrigue inside, with enough fascinating experiments to fill a few afternoons. Check out the Distorted Room where people go from midgets to megasize before your eyes. The Touch The Spring illusion blew me away—I kept calling strangers over to grab the coil that wasn't there. The

Antigravity Mirror was totally weird (look, I'm flying!), and if you're into microbes and fungi, you can hunt for the infinitesimal beasties under powerful video microscopes—who knew there was all this action in a drop of pond water?

And don't freak out if an experiment puzzles you. There's an incredibly helpful staff of groovy geeks on hand (not a pocket protector in sight) to demonstrate everything. Generally, activities are fast and easy to execute, so kids can try a lot in a little time. The Hall is also less hectic and crowded than the Liberty Science Center (see page 52), especially if you arrive after school groups leave.

Already ranked as one of the top ten science museums in the United States, the Hall added to its status in the late 1990s when it opened the KIDPOWER Science Playground—the largest in the country. This colorful collection of outdoor educational contraptions is so wildly imaginative, no one under eighty should miss it. High points include a twenty-five-foot seesaw for school group teeter-tottering, a giant pinball machine, metal xylophones you whack with rubber mallets, a sun catcher exhibit using mirrors to aim sunbeams and hit targets, plus a huge elevated energy wave that surfs back and forth for 120 feet. And I'm proud to say I was the first person ever to climb the red rope web of the Space Net tensile structure—to the top!

COOL KID'S CORNER: You'll find a watery exhibit at the Hall of Science where you can make giant bubbles. Here's the same soapy formula they use at the Hall so you can whip up some bubble juice at home: Put 2/3 cup of liquid dishwashing soap (Dawn or Joy are best) in 1 gallon of water. Add 1 tablespoon of glycerin and let the solution age for five days. Presto, bubble mania!

New York Transit Museum

**Address: Corner of Boerum Place and
Schermerhorn Streets, Brooklyn
Phone: 718-243-8601 • Ideal Age Group: 5 to 12
Admission: $3 adults/$1.50 children
Web site: www.mta.nyc.ny.us/museum**

D uring one of my first excursions into Manhattan, I begged my parents to take me on the subway, such was my fascination with the underground train. I was hooked by the simple novelty of holding my own token and dropping it in the turnstile. When the subway finally rolled into the station, its deafening noise rattled my untrained ears and I freaked out. Luckily, I can now ride the IRT without any parents in tow.

Today whenever out-of-town friends visit, their children always ask to ride the subway. So we do. We walk up to the front of the first car where we share space with other kids watching the eerie black of the subway tunnel racing by.

But I've discovered an even better place for a concentrated dose of subway sensations—the New York Transit Museum. The first hint that this is unlike any museum you've ever seen, is its location in an authentic, decommissioned IND station in Brooklyn. For the price of a token (double that for you) children can pass through the turnstiles into this subterranean shrine to commuting, renovated in 2002.

If you think about it, the subway is an incredible achievement—hundreds of miles of track dug through rock and dirt and mud by 30,000 men using not much more than picks, shovels, and strong immigrant backs. This amazing construction feat is well documented at the Transit Museum, where you can hear stories about diggers sucked out of underground tunnels and blown into the air. But the major attraction here is downstairs in the tube (with its live, 600-watt third rail), the home of nineteen restored subway cars, dating from as far back as 1904 (when a token was 5¢). Kids can ring the bells on wooden cars with wicker seats, or pretend to be traveling to the 1934 World's Fair on cars painted in the official blue and orange exposition colors.

They have some aboveground mass transit vehicles here, too, including the sawed-off cabs from a pair of real New York City buses. Kids clamber up into the driver's seats behind huge steering wheels to peer through the classic fishbowl windows. On the newer bus, I was able to push the overhead route destination buttons with a satisfying high-pitched beep. You'll also find original MTA conductor badges for sale in the gift shop, along with other authentic subway memorabilia and the best collection of children's train books ever gathered in one place.

COOL KID'S CORNER: Before they had subways in Brooklyn, horses pulled buses along tracks. These fast-moving omnibuses were dangerous to passing pedestrians who often had to leap out of the way, earning Brooklyn residents the name Dodgers. You guessed it—that's what they called Brooklyn's only professional baseball team until 1958 when they became the Los Angeles Dodgers.

New York Waterway Sightseeing Cruises

Address: Pier 78 at West 38th Street on the Hudson River
Phone: 1-800-533-3779 • Ideal Age Group: 5 to 12
Admission: $19 adults /$9 children
Web site: www.nywaterway.com

Circumnavigating the city by boat is an excellent way to get an initial overview (or water view) of this gigantic theme park before immersing kids in the real life adventure. It's so popular, in fact, that many out-of-town families arriving in New York head directly to the terminals of several river cruise companies docked on the Hudson River.

But I must post a warning. The oldest and best-known of the circle-the-city cruise lines offers a three-hour tour that could have been masterminded by Gilligan for the way it leaves children stranded. Three hours is an awfully long time when you're little. But one cruise line—N.Y. Waterway Sightseeing Cruises—seems to understand the tolerance level of five- to twelve-year-olds, and has created an excursion that abbreviates the trip to a kid-manageable ninety minutes. You won't completely circle Manhattan Island, but you'll enjoy all the highlights children want to see—the Empire State Building, the Statue of Liberty, the United Nations complex, and the Brooklyn Bridge.

N.Y. Waterway Cruises also offers a free shuttle bus service for families staying in midtown that conveniently drops you off at their sightseeing terminal at West Thirty-eighth Street, where you'll find a number of clean, comfortable, modern ferries. As the high-speed boat departs, take a seat on the left side of the upper deck (outside deck if it's sunny) for the best views of the passing skyline.

Knowledgeable and friendly guides pack a lot of fascinating city history into the water tour, with just enough silly trivia to hold a child's interest. And I like this cruise for another reason. A lot of tourists feel compelled to take their kids to the Statue of Liberty; but, frankly, I think it's a destination that parents *think* kids should like, but few children actually do. The lines for both the Liberty Island Ferry and to climb the statue stairs are unbearably long, and you can consume an entire afternoon dragging a child around who's growing justifiably agitated. Many kids are content to see the Green Lady up close from the decks of a N.Y. Waterway Cruise, without stretching the limits of their fidgetiness on the crowded shores of Liberty Island.

COOL KID'S CORNER: Here's some of that silly trivia I was telling you about—did you know that if you take a Hudson River pier number and subtract forty, you can tell what street you're on? Or that the district name, TriBeCa, is short for for Triangle Below Canal Street? Or that the Brooklyn Bridge was built in 1883—ten years before cars were invented? I learned a lot on my N.Y. Waterway Cruise.

Our Name Is Mud

**Address: 59 Greenwich Avenue at corner of
7th Avenue and 11th Street
Phone: 647-7899 • Ideal Age Group: 6 to 12
Admission: From $2 to $60
Average is $15 for most craft projects**

The scene: a rainy summer Saturday, your five-year-old has just watched *Parent Trap* for the second time and appears to be rewinding for a third viewing, while your seven-year-old is having a fit, kicking the kitchen cabinets out of frustration and boredom. The challenge: find something to do, Mom, quick!

In a cheery storefront studio in the Village (plus three other Manhattan locations), Our Name Is Mud has been saving rainy days since 1996 with innovative, walk-in crafts for kids. Children and parents can select from more than 100 styles of earthenware mugs, teacups, plates, vases, bowls, napkin rings, piggy banks and candlesticks to create. Owner Lorrie Veasey eschews useless, apartment-cluttering figurines, so at Mud kids leave with functional creations, all dishwasher-safe and microwaveable.

The white bisque (clay) has already been fired once, and after your child paints, sponges, or stencils on decorations, he or she can watch the piece being dunked in glaze that will give it a high shine. Kids can also visit the basement kiln where Mud does a final firing, but since firings happen overnight, they won't be able to watch the process. Finally, a few days later, you pick up the finished piece—which may be the only drawback, since delayed gratification is a bummer for kids.

There are two trained ceramicists at Mud at all times offering gentle instruction and encouragement, but not interfering with a child's masterpiece. Recently, I watched an 8-year-old paint a ceramic bathroom tile which he insisted his dad was going to grout into the family bathroom—now that takes refrigerator art to a new level! All in all, the Mud experience ends up being a wonderful, do-it-yourself way for children to make a lasting and practical Mother's or Father's Day gift for about the cost of a week's allowance.

P.S. The pre-cast crafts experience is repeated at **The Painted Pot** in Brooklyn (339 Smith Street/Carroll Gardens/718-222-0334) where owner Lisa Meyer works hard to make art a positive family experience in her large, bright, relaxed space.

COOL KID'S CORNER: Get ready for the newest craft which arrived at Mud in 2001—fired glass! You'll be able paint onto pre-blown cups, drinking glasses, pitchers, and vases using a brush and safe, non-toxic glass paint, in dozens of bright colors. After the kiln firing, you'll have a great-looking glass gift. Hey, now they'll have to call themselves "Our Name Is Glass!"

The Panorama of the City of New York

Address: Queens Museum of Art,
Flushing Meadows Corona Park, Queens
Phone: 718-592-9700 • Ideal Age Group: 7 to 12
Admission: $5 adults, $2.50 children

I magine taking the entire City of New York—all five boroughs, every one of the 895,000 buildings, the parks, the rivers, the airports, the thirty-five major bridges—and shrinking it down to fit inside one big room. That's exactly what they did at the Panorama of the City of New York—the world's largest three-dimensional scale model, and an exact replica of Gotham.

The Panorama is simply so awesome that any child who has ever labored over a Legos creation approaches it with dropped jaw and wide eyes. It took 200 model makers, engineers, and draftsmen three years to build the Panorama, originally constructed as an exhibit for the 1964-65 World's Fair. The cityscape was updated in 1994 by the original builders (Lester & Associates) to include 60,000 changes and additions—so it probably includes your condominium, too.

At the World's Fair, 1,400 visitors a day viewed the expanse from tracked cars (one of which is on display) that simulated helicopter flight at heights of 3,000 to 20,000 feet.

Now you walk along an elevated ramp way with glass floors that runs along the perimeter of the 9,335 square foot model. One of the Panorama's best features, which always elicits oohs and ahhs from young visitors, is the Night Scene enhancement. Every few minutes the room lights dim and the city glows with 2,500 green, orange, red, and blue lights, augmented with special black light illumination. The entire effect is totally eerie and wonderful.

The first thing city kids will want to do is find their apartment building and their school, along with landmarks like Yankee Stadium, the Empire State Building (just fifteen inches tall at this 1 inch to 100-foot scale), and the Statue of Liberty (look below your feet along the west walkway). If you want an improved view, bring along some binoculars, or rent a small pair at the gift shop for $1—it's worth it.

COOL KID'S CORNER: There are three great things to look for while you're here: the miniature airplanes taking off and landing at La Guardia airport—see if you can follow them flying across the black night sky of the ceiling, too; the world's largest elevator—located in the lobby of the building, it was used to carry World's Fair tourists visiting the Panorama, and it's the size of a small apartment; finally, pick up the cool New York Story pop-up toy in the gift shop and hold Manhattan in the palm of your hand!

Playground for All Children

Address: 111-01 Corona Avenue,
Flushing Meadows Corona Park, Queens
Phone: 718-699-8283 • Ideal Age Group: 2 to 12
Admission: Free

When the Playground for All Children (PAC, for short) opened in 1984, it was the first outdoor facility in the world designed to provide integrated play for non-disabled children and children with disabilities. Built at a cost of nearly $4 million, this was a showplace facility, the prototype for playgrounds of its kind.

The blueprint was to be repeated in all five boroughs, but funds dried up and PAC remained the only specialized playground in the city until the 1992 opening of the **Asser Levy Recreation Center** in Manhattan (23rd Street at Asser Levy Place/447-2020). While providing a vital service, Asser Levy does not have the range of offerings available at PAC, especially after the playground's recent renovation.

"All children" means that the PAC playground has something for all kids, regardless of variation in age or abilities. In fact, you would be unable to distinguish most of the playground apparatus here from equipment in your own neighborhood park, unless you were a child with a disability. Then you would notice that the slide has special wide steps and low railings you can climb with arms only. You would appreciate the nature trail with signs in braille that describe the foliage and points of interest. You would realize that your wheelchair can go anywhere in this 3.5-acre play facility with, of course, unobstructed and easy access to the restrooms.

There are at least two attendants at all times, and you won't find more dedicated city workers anywhere. They understand the needs of these children, focus only on what they can do, are trained to provide extra assistance if necessary, and encourage every child to participate fully, no matter what the disability. The staff is particularly skilled at creating games and activities where healthy interaction and integration occurs between non-disabled and disabled children. It's not uncommon to see non-disabled kids pushing wheelchair-bound visitors around the base paths in a pickup game of softball, or cooperative art projects being created at the indoor crafts area.

Other highlights of this playground include four hand-operated swings with adult-sized seats—these aluminum and rubber, high-back chairs have foot restraints and seat belts, and can be pumped with a pull chain. There are also puppet shows starring disabled puppets in the amphitheater during summers months, and an immensely popular Water Wheel—a fully accessible wet play area that douses delighted kids in July and August.

COOL KID'S CORNER: This pioneering playground started the PAC Pack—a team of dogs used in an innovative Pet Assisted Therapy program at the playground. These gentle canines have pushed wheelchairs, helped kids on apparatus, and offered lots of love. One of the dogs, Ayla, was even trained to respond to

Playspace

Address: 2473 Broadway at 92nd Street
Phone: 769-2300 • Ideal Age Group: 1 to 6
Admission: $7.50 per child or adult
Web site: www.playspaceny.com

Jump, run, crawl, slide, skip, tumble, dig, push, wriggle, laugh, climb, touch, share, eat, peek, sing, tickle, hug, hum, hop. Well, that about sums up the life of a toddler, and gives you a good idea of what to expect at the city's best indoor playground for the under six crowd.

What makes Playspace so superior? You'll like it for the enthusiastic, helpful staff (they'll run out and buy a fresh pair of OshKosh in the wake of a hopeless soiling), the immaculate cleanliness (every toy is sterilized every night), the premium put on safety, and the natural bright light from floor-to-ceiling windows. Your child won't notice any of that—in fact, I predict a beeline to the huge sandbox (5,000 pounds of the white stuff, strained and sifted weekly), the colorful elevated labyrinth, the miniature stage loaded with tutus, hats and dress-up costumes, and the lock, latch, and hatch-covered Door Wall (finally, three-year-olds get to bust open every throw bolt and twist lock known to man).

Another reason why Playspace is so much fun for kids, while accommodating the needs of escorting parents, is that this 8,000-square-foot play area was designed by a parent, not a business person. Owner and creator Allen McCullough was at a loss some years back when his son needed a safe, clean, rain-or-shine alternative to apartment play. The Vermont native wanted to capture the best of small town life, and employed master playground builder, Sam Kornhauser, to make this concept a reality.

The two men actually sawed and hammered much of the natural wood play areas themselves, mixing special nontoxic stains to create soothing wine and mustard color motifs on exposed panels. The two levels of the handmade, suspended crawl bridge have lots of built-in secret places and kid-sized crannies to hide in. McCullough and Kornhauser tested all the crawl spaces themselves to ensure that parents could accompany toddlers through every tunnel and climbing structure—another one of those safety-first features that includes a couple of inches of rubber surfacing on the floors and thick carpet padding everywhere else.

But let's get back to the sheer joy of unstructured play for preschoolers. There are dozens of popular riding toys in the tidy parking lot, a light booth where kinetic kids can throw the flicker switch like crazy, a tree house, a bi-level construction area with a neat wrecking ball, and (I love this) the city's smallest climbing wall—very short and blanketed with carpet so you can leave your safety harnesses at home. It's also worth noting that the play staff here includes young men, giving children a secure place to interact with male role models.

COOL KID'S CORNER: How much sand can you stand? The very big sandbox at Playspace is filled with digging trucks, special sifters on the wall, plus all the pails, shovels, and rakes you can hold. If you want to play alone, the sandbox has a private clubhouse and a cozy foam cave in the corner.

The Real World

**Address: Rockefeller Park, Chambers Street
on the Hudson River
Phone: 416-5300 • Ideal Age Group: 2 to 12
Admission: Free**

Every so often, an artist is born who can live a lifetime without losing the instincts to create like a child. The imagination stays nimble and fresh. A playfulness remains. For those exceptional people, the world of fantasy is comfortable and real . . . while reality seems ridiculous.

Tom Otterness is just that sort of artist. And his Real World playground of absurd and comical creatures in Rockefeller Park speaks the visual language of children perfectly. It is impossible not to love Otterness' fairy-tale family of pint-sized busy bodies—a civilization of bronze smiley faces I call the "Pill Box" men (because of those hats). Swimming in a sea of oversized pennies—the artist's reference to the nearby Financial Center—these and all sorts of half-human, half-animal carnivalesque sculptures delight children of every age in their riverfront tiny town.

Otterness is a Kansas native (possible Oz influence here) whose highly recognizable sculptures have been commissioned for projects throughout the city, including an underworld creation for the Mass Transit Authority.

He likes to make public art because it reaches so many

people. He works in bronze because he says it gets polished when people touch it—that way he can tell which of his sculptures children love most. His genial Dodo bird is the frequently nuzzled playmate of countless toddlers just a few hundred yards away in the Rockefeller Playground (see page 86).

He's created so many crazy characters in the Real World, doing so many offbeat things, your eyes have to work overtime. At the north entrance, you'll spot a bulldog chained to a water fountain, barking at a cat who's watching a bird who's eyeing a worm. Over there is Humpty Dumpty on the violin. Nearby, two frogs are wrestling under a penny fountain. And everywhere the Pill Box men are making mischief.

You'll discover that the Real World is particularly well-suited to young children learning their numbers. There's a long winding Penny Path snaking through the playground with an alternating little feet motif. Children can step on the feet while counting pennies along the walkway for a game that fully engages little minds and bodies.

Cool Kid's Corner: Mr. Otterness has tucked some of his most magical sculptures in hard-to-see places. Can you find the cigar smoking turtle on the wall, the dark monk with a sickle sitting atop a light post, the gagged cat, the unplugged phone, and the man-snake reading on the pole? The first one to find all five wins!

Rockefeller Playground

**Address: Rockefeller Park, Vesey Street on the
Hudson River • Phone: 416-5300
Ideal Age Group: 2 to 10 • Admission: Free**

During research for this book, I spoke to dozens of parents and children about their favorite places to visit in New York. An astonishing number of fun-seeking informants named the Rockefeller Playground "the city's best playground." One family was so hooked, they visited regularly from Brooklyn to play here on weekends.

How, I wondered, could one cluster of slides, sandboxes, and jungle gyms gain such unanimous praise and stand so far above the rest? I went to find out—and I had to forcibly restrain myself from throwing off my jacket and dashing up the red climbing nets. Why do six-year-olds have all the fun?

One of the outstanding features of this playground is its idyllic setting on the waterfront, within twenty-five acres of continuous parks and gardens. At this open, airy environment, just steps from the surging Hudson, children bask in sunlight and sea breeze, features that contribute to an expansive play experience. In a city where children are too often confined to small, limited play areas, Rockefeller Playground says "You're free, go wild." And kids do.

To my eye, the playground is built as a microcosm of the city—with a maze of high-rise climbing structures, bridges, and towers looking down on the bustling activity of toddler play areas, hopscotch games, and sandboxes. This playground is also so safe, clean, and smartly designed, parents find they can temporarily relax their own vigilance and just let kids play. Opportunities abound for that.

At the south end is a cheerful red carousel for smaller children that parents can push or kids can pedal power. It travels slowly on its own circular track and always prompts a passing parade of smiling faces. Further on is a wooden-bowed bridge (run fast, make lots of banging sounds with your feet), firemen's sliding poles, a bright yellow spiral slide, a three-foot elevated sandbox for standing play, lots of swings, muscle-building climbing nets, and several springy jumpers. The expansive climbing area is clearly marked (9 AND OLDER, AGES 2–5, etc.), so parents can gauge apparatus difficulty with a child's skill level. The entire playground is also covered with a thick, spongy surface to cushion inevitable falls.

This state-of-the-art playground includes an amusing water play area where a big concrete hippo faces off with an undaunted elephant in a summer-long squirting duel. Four dog faces peer out of the adjacent east wall to get in on the spouting fun.

COOL KID'S CORNER: Bring your chalk. The bouncy black sur-face of the playground is really fun to draw on. Everywhere you look children have created chalk flowers, houses, colorful hop-ping paths, and chalk people, too.

Roosevelt Island Aerial Tram

Address: 59th Street and Second Avenue
Phone: 832-4543 • Ideal Age Group: 3 to 8
Admission: $3 round-trip

When you're looking for great places to take children, you've got to think like a child. Let's take the Roosevelt Island Tram, for instance. Now to most adults it's a practical, if not picturesque way to commute between the East River Island and Manhattan. But to a kid, the tram is a carnival ride, a bubble in the sky, a great way to fly!

Every fifteen minutes the aerial tram departs from Sixtieth Street and starts its three-and-a-half minute glide, 250 feet above the river on huge cables. For children, this experience is a major rush. The large, four-sided glass cable cars offer a way up high view of the towering skyscrapers of midtown. Kids love to watch the multicolored specks racing down the black ribbons of the avenues, while chubby tugboats push barges through the swirling river waters below.

There are a thousand things to see from the Roosevelt Island Tram and children notice it all: cars zipping by on the adjacent Queensboro Bridge, helicopters taking off from the Sixty-third Street Heliport, a police boat plying the waters near the Manhattan shoreline, a building fire trailing smoke somewhere far off in Brooklyn.

After this aerial sightseeing tour is over, the tram follows a steep slope into its docking descent and jerks to rest with a few bumps that always amuse little ones. Once off the cable car, walk your children over to the big window of the tram's engine room. You can peek inside to see the enormous yellow gears and the blue, orange, and green tinker toy interior. Was this place made for kids or what?

Don't quit now. This is a fun-filled little island that starts with a 25¢ ride on the red buses along Main Street. Ride to the northernmost stop where you and your children can step off, then continue to walk past the beautiful community gardens along the East River promenade to the child-sized, fifty-foot stone lighthouse at the island's tip. There's a wonderful sun-filled park for picnicking here, a fine place for quiet conversation with your kids (remember that?) away from the bustle of Manhattan. You'll probably see a handful of friendly fisherman and lots of seagulls, but few other island dwellers. The native Canarsie Indians called this little island Minnahannock, loosely translated as "It's Nice to Be on the Island." Yeah, sure, but who would want to miss the return ride to Manhattan on the tram?

COOL KID'S CORNER: Here's my favorite thing to do on the aerial tram. Watch for the other cable car passing by in the opposite direction. You'll meet at about midpoint and then you can make friendly, funny faces at the huddled commuters floating by!

Rose Center For Earth and Space

Address: Central Park West at 81st Street
Phone: 769-5200 for Space Show reservations
Ideal Age Group: 8 to 12 • Admission: $12 adults/$7 children
(suggested)/or with Space Show admission $21 adults and
$12.50 children • Web site: www.amnh.org

The gleaming cube of glass is so bright and breathtaking, the four-million pound Hayden Sphere hovering inside it is so massive and magnificent, you just know that the Rose Center for Earth and Space is going to be astonishing, sensational, spectacular. And you're never disappointed.

The Rose Center, opened in 2000, is part of the American Museum of Natural History (page 16), and your ticket to the museum gains you access to this new facility. But I've included it as a separate location not only because the scope of the astronomical science here deserves to stand alone, but also because it's a bad idea to hustle children through both exhibition-rich venues in a day. There's just too much good stuff you're going to miss, and that would be a shame for the entire family.

I started my afternoon at the Rose Center with a group of sixth-grade science students watching an engrossing short film about Black Holes. We learned why they call these matter-sucking celestial bodies "gravity's ultimate triumph," and tensed when the narrator said we'd reached "the edge of no return." Yipes!

The Hall of Planet Earth included the world's oldest known rock as well as the Earth Event Wall with television broadcasts on global earthquakes and volcanoes as they happen. You can even create your own mini-earthquake by jumping on a bull's-eye painted on the floor and measuring your impact on the seismometer needle nearby.

The Heilbrunn Cosmic Pathway, a gently sloping 360-foot walkway that orbits the Hayden Sphere, leads you on an exploration of 13 billion years of cosmic evolution. Want to feel small? I learned that although it looks quite tiny from here, the Sun is actually so big you could fit one million planet Earths inside of it!

The completely rebuilt Hayden Planetarium, housed in the Hayden Sphere, is where the center's most thrilling attraction happens; the multi-sensory Space Show, *Passport to the Universe*, narrated by Tom Hanks. Using the world's largest and most powerful virtual-reality simulator, your seat shakes and vibrates as you lift off on a million-mile-per-hour journey past planets, star clusters, and galaxies. This invigorating, hyper-realistic space flight to the edge of the observable universe was created using the latest astronomical observations and galactic computer models from NASA and the Hubble Space Telescope. It's a one-of-a-kind show that's as "far out" and mind-expanding as any entertainment experience on the planet.

COOL KID'S CORNER: If you're feeling chubby, just step on the lunar scale and see how ultra-light you'd be on the moon. Digital scales imbedded in the floor of the Hall of the Universe will also reveal your weight on Saturn, Jupiter, a neutron star, and the Sun. No need to lose weight … just travel to the stars!

Smithsonian's National Museum of the American Indian

Address: 1 Bowling Green, across from Battery Park
Phone: 514-3888 • Ideal Age Group: 6 to 12
Admission: Free • Web site: www.si.edu/nmai

I've always been moved by the Native American philosophy regarding the seventh generation—that whatever we do today, we should consider it's impact on the seventh generation of our children. Its probably naive to romanticize the traditions and history of indigenous peoples, but they do have something to teach us about the delicate balance between people and nature, spirituality and art, and respect for family and elders.

At the beautifully curated American Indian museum, children are exposed to some of the intricate crafts, powerful music, old stories, and native objects that say so much about the people of these fascinating cultures. These exhibits are made even more riveting and dramatic by the museum's location in a magnificent landmark building—the old U.S. Custom House, a Beaux Arts masterpiece built just after the turn of the century (mention to your children that the main rotunda on the second floor, with its oval skylight and detailed ceiling murals, is used in many Hollywood movies).

The Smithsonian has nearly one million Native

American artifacts in its collection with only a small percentage on display here. Still, there's no shortage of stone carvings, weavings, blankets, baskets, pottery, and jewelry in the winding galleries. Leather fighting shields, feathered war bonnets, and scary dance masks always get a child's attention, although much of these items appear behind glass cases, off-limits to curious young hands. There are a few touchable items, most notably a thick buffalo-skin robe that evokes snowy scenes from the classic *Dances with Wolves*. I also liked the constant chanting and drumming of tribal music piped through the space, which heightens the mystery and intensity.

Very young children will tire quickly of the artifacts displays, which require easy but sometimes extensive reading. They'll be happier in front of the video screens featuring legends, myths, and stories told by contemporary chiefs and elders, both men and women. The Resource Center also has interactive touch screens with age appropriate activities. Finally, the museum features an Especially For Kids film series twice a day, focusing on the lives of today's Native American youngsters.

I saw the largest number of children clustered near the Round Dance Exhibit, a display incorporating dozens of pairs of colorfully-beaded moccasins, all arranged in a circle, left foot up, as if the wearers were mid-step in a ritual pow-wow dance. It gave me chills.

COOL KID'S CORNER: You can buy authentic Native American turquoise jewelry and silver work, beaded leather vests, feathered headdresses, and drumming music in the first floor gift shop. Also, be sure to visit the Resource Center where they have tribal newspapers like the *Navajo Times* and *Seminole Tribune* sent from reservations.

Socrates Sculpture Park

**Address: Broadway at Vernon Boulevard,
Long Island City, Queens • Phone: 718-956-1819
Ideal Age Group: 5 to 12 • Admission: Free**

Too much art in too many pretentious settings can discourage a kid. I had the misfortune of plunking myself down in a giant leather baseball mitt at the Guggenheim once, and was soundly chastised by a museum guard (she actually called me a "dummy"). Hey, I couldn't help it, the impulse just came over me.

No such problem for energetic souls at the Socrates Sculpture Park. Children of all ages are encouraged to touch, hang from, climb over, and sit on dozens of large-scale sculptures in this 4 1/2-acre waterfront park. The inspiration of Queens steel-girder sculptor, Mark di Suvero, this unassuming sculpture garden was an illegal garbage dump for years, until it was reclaimed and revitalized by the artist and his neighbors in 1985.

Not that Socrates Park has forgotten its humble beginnings. You can still find a piece of rusted wire here, a butane tank in the bushes over there, an old oil drum tossed by a storm fence. But overall the former rubble strewn lot offers a kind of rugged sanctuary from the oily garages, welding shops, and masonry warehouses on Vernon Boulevard. It's okay to run, play, throw a ball, or picnic in the shadow of Socrates' towering wood, stone, and steel creations by both well-known and emerging artists. It's a particularly smart excursion with children on hot days when the East River breezes cool off the shoreline and circulate the five melodious tones of the windmill-like sculpture titled Wind Gamelan.

Feeling climby? Two curious sculptures, the satellite silhouette of The Cloak of Motion and the neon green top of the aluminum and Plexiglas Resurrection bridge, rival the best outdoor playground apparatus. Children always spot the green, wood-carved snake slithering up the sculpted tree above Socrates' office trailer, too—just another inch and it will finally gulp down that egg. Another favorite pastime for children here is locating their initials in the granite alphabet wall that borders the park on the east side. Exhibits change with regularity, too, so there's always something new looming before you.

Besides its dramatic physical setting, and the interactive nature of its sculptures, Socrates is unusual in another respect. Children have the opportunity to meet artists working on-site. Watching sculptors create their pieces with rock-crushing jackhammers and white hot torches never fails to impress kids who tend to believe that all art is made in genteel studios with delicate brushes and tools.

COOL KID'S CORNER: Along the eastern fence of Socrates Park lies the sculpture, Vanishing, with 300 endangered species pictured on ceramic tile blocks—everything from frogs to deer to ducks to snakes to shellfish. See how many different animals you can find and name, or bring your school class here to identify imperiled species you'll help protect one day.

Sony 3-D IMAX Theatre

Address: 68th Street at Broadway
Phone: 336-5020 • Ideal Age Group: 6 to 12
Admission: $10 adults /$6.50 children

Everything at the Sony IMAX Theatre is big. And kids love big.

There's a big movie screen (among the largest in the country and the planet), a big sound system (18,000 watts of surround sound), and big 3-D action (stampeding buffaloes as big as bulldozers, frolicking fish the size of freighters). Just taking the escalators past the seventy-five-foot Hollywood mural up to the 600-seat theatre is a big experience.

But, without a doubt, the coolest part of IMAX for children is the futuristic headset they issue you as you step through the theatre door. Forget those outdated scenes from the 1950s of a stiff, formally dressed audience watching 3-D movies wearing cardboard sunglasses. Totally unique to this theatre experience are lightweight, heavy-duty plastic goggles that look like a cross between a welder's mask and virtual-reality headgear. With my pair firmly over my face I felt like Luke Skywalker in *Star Wars*, and I didn't want to take them off (but I had to—each pair gets a thorough cleaning and disinfecting before the next show begins).

Once you've finished laughing at the bizarre look these

wraparound 3-D headsets give the rest of your family, you can lean back in the comfy seats for the IMAX movie. IMAX is the world's largest film format (ten times larger than 35mm) which enables the theatre to project a monstrous image onto a screen the size of an eight-story building—eighty-feet-high by one-hundred-feet-wide. Add to that the most advanced, electronic 3-D technology, and you're sitting at the edge of your seat watching movie images that surround you, crawl into your lap, almost sneak up behind you. Invariably, you also see lots of little hands reaching out to snatch passing 3-D images from the air (okay, I did it, too).

The Sony IMAX Theatre is one of the first 3-D theaters in the nation to feature full-length classics being released in this format, *Beauty and the Beast* and *Fantasia* among them. And while 95 percent of the 3-D film offerings here are G-rated, they also have spectacular concert films like *All Access* for teens and adults, and the environmentally significant, *Galapagos*.

COOL KID'S CORNER: Besides showing big 3-D movies, this Sony Theatre complex is also the site of big movie premieres. My nephew, Zach, was up from Florida once when we saw Eddie Murphy pull up in a long black stretch limo for a movie opening here. Eddie walked right up to him, winked, and shook his hand. Zach told everybody about it for weeks and still says it was the best thing that ever happened to him in New York.

Sony Wonder Technology Lab

Address: 550 Madison Avenue at 56th Street
Phone: 833-8100 • Ideal Age Group: 6 to 12
Admission: Free • Web site: www.sonywondertechlab.com

Connecting high tech with high touch is the idea behind Sony Wonder, where children become media trainees and get to explore all the newest eye-popping communications technology coming out of the company's cutting edge computer and video labs.

It's hard to imagine that Sony would assemble this futuristic cyber station in the first place, much less make it available free to the public. But here it is, four floors of electronic playground and digital adventure, and if Sony wants to throw in a few plugs for its products for the visitation privileges, that's cool with me.

You're greeted at the ground floor elevators by young Sony staffers (called "Explainers") clad in black jumpsuits with requisite walkie-talkies, and already you're hooked by the promise of something sensational. Next you're handed a Sony Wonder Card and whisked up to the Log-In Station— a kind of darkened, intergalactic star world rigged with eight video prompts. At log-in you hear a chorus of male and female voices beckoning you to the video screens, "Come here, over here." Then you follow your on-screen guides to have the Wonder Card magnetically encoded with your name, image, and voice imprint. The card now becomes your pass for activating exhibits. (Hint: When the camera locks onto your image make a funny face for repeated laughs every time you swipe the card.)

Yahoo! Now you can descend the chrome and neon ramps into three more floors of fun. First I stopped at ROVER (Remote Operated Video Enhanced Robot) to manipulate a giant robotic arm in an attempt to find a dangerous radioactive leak—I broke a sweat. Next it was on to the Audio Lab, where I sat at a jazzy console with other media trainees and created a bizarre musical composition. Then, at the Image Lab, my funny face was projected on a screen before me and using a handheld Power Tracker gun, I electronically painted, pinched, and ultimately turned my image into a monstrous mosaic.

Sony Wonder Technology Lab also has a working television studio that gives children a chance to play camera operator and director. But the ultimate charge for most kids is the PlayStation, an area stocked with the latest 3-D video games. After being KO'd repeatedly in an incredibly realistic kung-fu kicking duel, I reluctantly handed over my joystick to an eight-year-old breathing down my neck.

COOL KID'S CORNER: Say hello to b.b. Wonderbot – the bug-eyed, remote-controlled robot who'll meet you at the entrance to Sony Wonder. He has miniature television cameras hidden in his eyeballs and microphones implanted in his faceless head to see and hear all. Once inside the lab, you'll get a peak at the virtual reality gadgetry behind this amusing, lifelike robot.

South Street Seaport Buskers

Address: 19 Fulton Street
Phone: 732-7678 • Ideal Age Group: 2 to 12
Admission: Free to marketplace/Fees vary for museums
Web site: www.southstreetseaport.com

F amilies are helping to revitalize lower Manhattan by visiting one of our most exciting historical neighborhoods which offers a fascinating square mile of fulfilling outings: there's the four, well-marked Heritage Trails for exploring the Colonial settlement of New Amsterdam; a rich schedule of summer-long free family performances in Hudson and Battery Parks; or you can take your child on a scenic, hour-long, round-trip boat ride through New York Harbor aboard the big orange and blue Staten Island Ferry for free!

But for sheer entertainment, there's no better bet than a visit to the eleven square blocks of restored nineteenth-century buildings known as the South Street Seaport. Dating back to the 1600s, the Seaport district now draws more than 10 million people a year to its maritime museum, street-level retail shops, and thirty-plus restaurants. There's a small Children's Center with hands-on exhibits all related to waterfront life and sea voyaging where kids can rock on a heavy mast to experience the fury of strong seas. Children of every age are also drawn to the Seaport's historic tall ships. Climb aboard the landmark *Peking*—a 347-foot, four-masted giant that's the second-largest sailing ship in the world today. Or cast off for a two-hour sail on the century-old schooner *Pioneer*, where children can help raise the sails or even take the helm (the *Pioneer* sails seasonally).

In my opinion, the single most appealing children's attraction at the Seaport is the incredible concentration of buskers, or street performers. During the warm months, the Seaport encourages street artists to entertain along the cobblestone pedestrian walkways, and these talented artists arrive in droves. What results is an amazingly vibrant carnival, a street circus, a colorful world of jugglers, magicians, mimes, musicians, puppeteers, and balloon sculptors. And all this entertainment is free.

One summer Sunday I listened to a guitarist play a medley of Neil Young tunes, a magician struggle to rip himself free of a straitjacket in under two minutes, an acrobat juggle knives while another swallowed fire, and a comedian do twenty minutes of G-rated material. In fact, the children were laughing hardest.

COOL KID'S CORNER: Look for the green-painted lady posing as a stone-still Statue of Liberty, the young piano virtuoso playing Beethoven on a portable keyboard while his father collects the change, and the silent balloon twister skillfully sculpting rubber animals for a dollar. There are so many weird and wacky buskers at the Seaport, you may have to come back again tomorrow.

The Swedish Cottage
Marionette Theater

Address: Central Park, enter at West 81st Street
Phone: 988-9093 • Ideal Age Group: 4 to 10
Admission: $6 adult/$5 children, reservations required

You walk through the woods, skip along a flower-edged pathway, then stumble upon a small wooden cottage nestled next to a beautiful garden. You climb a few steps, open the door, and look up to see dozens of silent marionettes hanging along exposed rafters—there's a princess over there, a wizard over your head, an Indian in feathered headdress suspended above the doorway. What sort of fantasy place is this? What kind of magic happens here?

You've discovered the charming Swedish Cottage Marionette Theater—a cozy place just a hundred yards walk from Central Park West that has introduced generations of New York children to the wonders of live puppet theater. Originally built in Sweden for the 1876 Centennial Fair in Philadelphia, and later brought to the New York, the peak-roofed, arch-windowed baltic fir structure served a host of functions before 1973, when it began to house puppet productions.

Scaled down to kid-size, this sweet theater has rows of curved, low benches facing a gold-curtained stage. The colorful sets are marvelously elaborate and creative, the ornate marionettes (each a couple feet tall) are finely crafted and expressive, and the sophisticated puppet work here is deft, polished, and beautiful to watch. The cottage produces a new show every year (with a two-week break in July and a one-month hiatus in September), always a classic fairy tale such as Cinderella, Peter Pan, or Jack and the Beanstalk, and always with an urban twist. When I went to see Sleeping Beauty, for instance, her royal family lived in Central Park's Belvedere Castle and the African-American god-fairy sang gospel tunes and imparted wisdom laced with inner-city jargon. It was brilliant.

Typically, there's an amusing, five-minute introduction from a member of the puppeteer crew, when he or she demonstrates the workings of a marionette and then asks audience members to help wake the puppets sleeping behind the curtain with a collective scream. The friendly puppeteers reappear after the show to answer questions. Always patient, they seem well aware that these one-hour performances are often a small child's first exposure to theater of any kind.

New York has other excellent puppet theaters for children. **PuppetWorks** (338 Sixth Avenue at 4th Street, Park Slope/718-965-3391) is locally famous for thirty-five years of traditional marionette productions at its storefront theater in Brooklyn's historic district. And you'll be guaranteed a world-class puppet performance at the **Lenny Suib Puppet Playhouse** (555 East 90th Street at York Avenue/369-8890).

COOL KID'S CORNER: After a visit to The Swedish Cottage lots of kids want to put on puppet shows of their own. If that's you, then visit **DINOSAUR HILL** (306 East 9th Street at 2nd Avenue/473-5850), a puppet palace with hundreds of hand and finger puppets, plus high-quality marionettes—unicorns, clowns, magicians and villains—made especially for kids, with color-coded strings that untangle in a jiffy.

TADA!

**Address: 15 West 28th Street, 2nd floor, bet.
Broadway and Fifth Avenue • Phone: 627-1732
Ideal Age Group: 5 to 12
Admission: 10-week classes start at $260
Web site: www.tadatheater.com**

This is a city for entertainers, with hundreds of Broadway plays, cabarets, staged readings, and musical concerts going up every night. Talented actors, singers, dancers, and performers of every size, shape, and vocal range are giving their all to make audiences laugh, cry, and vibrate with excitement. It's electrifying stuff, and if you're a little person growing up here you can't help but be affected; you've got to wonder if maybe, just maybe, there isn't a little bit of star in you.

Well, raise the curtain and turn on the footlights, because I know the perfect place to find out—TADA! This unique theater company and performance school gives kids a place to develop their voice, dance, and stage techniques in a safe, supportive, upbeat environment. And TADA! is exclusively for children—in fact, it's New York's only youth theater ensemble, with classes and productions that are relevant to kids.

Young performers from every ethnic and socioeconomic background come here to hone dramatic skills, learn improvisation, and play theater games (in the five-to-six-year-old classes, children also make simple masks, props, and puppets to use in shows). And as it turns out, many of the city's finest professional actors aren't waiting tables, they're teaching at TADA!. Every after-school and Saturday class (maximum of twenty children) is taught by a choreographer/director and a musical director—so even the more introverted students get attention.

Each class semester ends with an exuberant performance for families and friends in TADA!'s very own ninety-five-seat theater (hey, this is showbiz). Many children in the musical theater school then try out in open auditions to become a member of TADA!'s ensemble troupe, which puts on three high-quality, original productions a year.

Watching a class of eight- to twelve-year-olds in TADA!'s rehearsal space, I was reminded of a humiliating experience I had in the third grade singing an "Edelweiss" solo in an assembly. I thought I'd pulled it off quite well, but was later mocked by the music teacher for a few squeals on the high notes. End of singing career. You can be sure there's nothing like that going on at TADA!. The instructors I saw were positively thrilled with every sung note and dance step, and the kids all seemed to shine in the generous spotlight. I was also amazed at the camaraderie between these preteens, with the more confident kids pulling the wallflowers, well . . . off the wall.

COOL KID'S CORNER: I thought you might like to hear part of a poem written by a kid like you who was excited to be performing at TADA!, "I shouted, I screamed, I strutted, I pranced, did cartwheels and flips and sang and danced, for I had just gotten the best news so far, that I would belong to a place called, TADA!"

Tah-Poozie

Address: 50 Greenwich Street bet. Sixth and Seventh Aves.
Phone: 647-0668 • Ideal Age Group: 3 to 12
Admission: Free

Remember going down to the local five-and-dime when you were a kid and buying an excellent toy with your allowance money that you'd play with nonstop for a week—a balsa-wood glider with a rubber-band engine and a red plastic propeller, or a superball that you could bounce over the roof?

In a world of hundred-and-fifty-dollar Playstations and hundred-dollar skateboards, it's hard for a city kid to find true toy satisfaction for just a few bucks. Unless you take your child (along with a few of his or her best friends) to Tah-Poozie.

Shmuel Kerhaus has been filling every wall of his narrow Village store with affordable fun since 1988, and he knows what makes children happy. Kids go absolutely wild here sifting through shelves upon colorful shelves of toys and games and gizmos, most priced from 50 cents to six dollars, and all thoughtfully placed near a child's eye level.

Shmuel gave me the toy tour recently, complete with nonstop demonstrations, which kept us both laughing. Check out the wild wind-up dinosaurs and pigs, the acrobatic aliens, the assortment of squirting spiders and fish, sticky eyeballs, rainbow viewers, and tiny animals that grow gigantic inside soda bottles. I picked up a childhood favorite—Magic Rocks—along with a pocket-sized periscope ideal for snooping around corners. Shmuel also has gobs of glow-in-the-dark jewelry, jiggly glow snakes, creepy spiders, and all sorts of neon Slinkies, all of which makes Tah-Poozie a prime spot for picking party bag favors.

I'm a frequent visitor to another must-see toy store. The **Enchanted Forest** (925-6677/85 Mercer Street between Spring and Broome Streets) has a giant tree and hanging walkway inside, with nostalgic retro playthings that are as fun for kids now as they were when you were young.

COOL KID'S CORNER: At Tah-Poozie they have the best collection of flip books anywhere with samples of all the zippy scenes for you to try. I was mesmerized by Stunt Auto (crash!), The Cat and the Butterfly (swipe! swat!), Jumping Dolphin (swish!), and the History of Flight (wheee!). Did you know that this is exactly how movies are made? One picture frame at a time, moving quickly past your eyes.

Tannen's Magic Studio

**Address: 24 West 25th Street bet. Sixth Avenue
and Broadway, 2nd floor
Phone: 929-4500 • Ideal Age Group: 5 to 12
Admission: Free**

Hocus Pocus! Abracadabra! Simsalabim! These are the magic words. Children all over the world learn them almost as soon as they can talk, and every time they're spoken there's the anticipation of something fantastic about to happen, something amazing and wonderful.

As it turns out, the world's epicenter for constant quakes of magical excitement is right here in New York, at Tannen's Magic Studio. The largest magic shop on the planet, with more than 7,800 tricks and illusions in stock, has been a mecca for amateur and professional magicians for more than sixty years. New Jersey native, David Copperfield, got his start at Tannen's purchasing card tricks as a teenager. Siegfried and Roy bought their first illusions from Tannen's first owner, Lou Tannen, thirty years ago. Dick Cavett, a master at sleight of hand, is a regular customer. Even Muhammad Ali, a magic nut, has shopped here.

For children, a visit to Tannen's is like every birthday party they've ever been to rolled into one. The moment they step into the store, they are surrounded, floor to ceiling, with the countless colorful props that make every magic show so unforgettable—silk scarves, magic wands, shiny coins, big top hats, mysterious black boxes, startling straitjackets, razor-sharp swords, dangling ropes, and decks upon decks of rigged playing cards. Even the most jaded child could spend an hour here transfixed by the mesmerizing faces of the ventriloquist dummies in the front display case.

And there's an added bonus with every trip to Tannen's—you get to see live magic every minute. That's because current owner Tony Spina and all the folks behind the counter are professional magicians. They're here to demonstrate the coin magic, illusions, and card tricks that prospective customers have come to buy. And kids can watch.

Tannen's has some excellent beginner magic sets for children seven and older that offer a dozen simple tricks for under thirty dollars. Three marvelous tricks you can ask for—magic that kids love and can master easily—are Spooky (the floating spirit silk), Scotch 'N Soda (a half dollar and copper coin switch), and the Magic Coloring Book. My suggestion is that you let younger children enjoy the illusion of magic as long as possible, and leave the starter sets for slightly older kids.

COOL KID'S CORNER: Look up when you enter Tannen's. See all those playing cards stuck to the ceiling? They're part of an amazing trick called "Card on the Ceiling," which the staff magicians will perform for you. And when you get a little older, you'll be ready to learn other mind-bending tricks on sale here, like the Bohemian Torture Escape, Twisting Head, Girl into Lion, and the Buzzsaw Illusion!

Winnie-the-Pooh at Donnell Library Center

Address: 20 West 53rd Street bet. Fifth and Sixth Avenues
Phone: 212-621-0636 • Ideal Age Group: 2 to 12
Admission: Free

I hadn't discovered the reassuring sweetness of the Winnie-the-Pooh books until my late twenties, a time when my life had become anxiety-filled and difficult. Quite by accident, I stumbled upon A. A. Milne's 1920s children's classics, and read myself to sleep with Pooh and his friends for months. The "bear of little brain" made me smile, and tiny Piglet's vulnerability made me cry. I could empathize with Eeyore's gloominess — I was feeling the same way — while longing for Tigger's bounciness and Kanga's mothering. Spending time in the calming rhythms of the Hundred Acre Wood healed me, and I'm grateful for it.

What's quite astonishing is that many children today don't know that the hero of the series, Christopher Robin, was modeled on A. A. Milne's son Christopher, and whose cherished stuffed-animal family inspired the Pooh characters. What's even more amazing is that five of Christoper Milnes's original toy companions (including Pooh) left England in 1947 and now reside permanently here in New York at the Donnell Library's Central Children's Room.

You can't help but feel awed and excited as you step off the second-floor elevator and approach the famous characters of Tigger, Kanga, Pooh, Eeyore, and Piglet, sitting in a climate-controlled glass case. Oh, what I'd give to cuddle with the Pooh bear for just a minute or two.

It's clear that Christopher Robin loved his plush pals well—Piglet's fur has been hugged right down to the leather, Kanga's neck has been squeezed so hard it has required several surgeries, and Eeyore wears more than one reparative patch. But it's the sight of Pooh, sitting nobly in the center, that makes your heart skip a beat. This is not the Disney-animation Pooh, not a cheap stuffed imitation Pooh, but the original Edward Bear who went "bump, bump, bump" down the stairs behind Christopher Robin. Be sure to sign Pooh's guest book, which contains the names of thousands of other children and adult fans from around the world who have already sworn their devotion.

COOL KID'S CORNER: Press your nose to the display glass and look closely at the downcast Eeyore. You'll see a very fine netting over his body applied by museum curators trying to protect the weary gray donkey. Nearby, you can also see the parakeet-topped parasol owned by *Mary Poppins* creator P. L. Travers; several rabbit figurines donated by *Peter Rabbit* author Beatrix Potter; and original paper cuts by Hans Christian Andersen of *Ugly Duckling* fame—all part of the rare and enchanting children's book collection housed here.

16 More Great Places
To Take Kids.

Just For the Fun of It!

Belvedere Castle
Address: Mid-Central Park at 81st Street
Ideal Age Group: 4 to 12 • Admission: Free

To get a sense of the impact that Belvedere Castle has on the imaginations of little minds, stand on the first-level terrace and watch children approach. At about a hundred paces they all break into an uncontrolled run, eager to explore this regal medieval-like structure in Central Park. Built as a lookout in 1872 to provide visitors with beautiful, unobstructed views of the park, it has been restored to its nineteenth-century splendor after years of neglect. For children, the castle is a storybook come to life. There's a moat (the Turtle Pond), ramparts (the stone outcropping it sits on), parapets, turrets, a dragon crest over the door, and a narrow circular staircase leading to the main tower. Open year-round, there are excellent, interactive nature exhibits here that kids like, but the real appeal of Belvedere Castle is simply as a backdrop for fantasy play. Take a seat on a sunny balcony, and let your kids get into their Renaissance Fair.

Biking The New York Greenway

Address: Battery Park to 132nd Street
Ideal Age Group: 5 to 12 • Admission: Free

It was my blue Schwinn Stingray with the silver-metallic banana seat, the two-foot sissy bar, and the five-speed stick shift that launched my obsession with biking. My first bike was also my first foray into freedom. But where does a Manhattan kid find a place to ride safely close to home? The spectacular New York Greenway system, opening miles of riverfront to experienced bikers and little tikers, is the answer. Right now, the best completed stretch of this landscaped esplanade is along the Hudson River. Smooth, paved paths keep you safely away from motorized traffic as you and your child pass notable sights like enormous yachts, miniature golf courses, helicopter pads, kayak boathouses, ferry boat terminals, and the massive Intrepid aircraft carrier. But for most kids, it's the simple memory of biking for miles with Mom or Dad that will never be forgotten.

Bowlmor Lanes

Address: 110 University Place bet. 12th and 13th Streets
Phone: 255-8188 • Ideal Age Group: 6 to 12
Admission: $5.95 per person per game/$4 for shoes
(no children after 6 P.M.) • Web site: www.bowlmor.com

Gone are the days of boring white pins and plain black balls. At Bowlmor Lanes the satisfying sound of heavy orbs crashing against ten sitting ducks is accompanied by techno-color innovations—neon green, yellow, orange, and red pins, balls of every hue (and lightweight ones for little people), plus a first-rate sound system. A major spiffing up at Bowlmor in the late '90s has brought out a new breed of bowler—young and hip. Kids love the loud pop music, the good snack food, the cool shoes, and the probability of spotting a celebrity bowler (lots of famous types in the neighborhood). In fact, Bowlmor keeps autographed pins in the display cases from recent guests like The Backstreet Boys and Lenny Kravitz, actors Liv Tyler and Ethan Hawke, plus comedian Conan O'Brien. Bowling bashes are good for birthdays, too, and at Bowlmor they throw a strike when it comes to children's parties.

Brooklyn Children's Museum

**Address: 145 Brooklyn Avenue and
St. Mark's Avenue, Brooklyn
Phone: 718-735-4400 • Ideal Age Group: 2 to 12
Admission: $4 per person
Web site: www.brooklynkids.org**

The world's first museum created just for children knows a few things about keeping kids entertained and interested. Founded in 1899, BCM pioneered the concept of participatory exhibits, and kids have had their hands occupied ever since. Noted for its subterranean architecture (from street level, all you see is a bunker-type entrance and some bumps in the lawn), the museum's single most compelling feature is the corrugated metal tunnel—a reclaimed drainage pipe—which descends through four levels of the underground structure. This neon-lit people tube has a 120-foot stream running down its middle with paddle wheels, sluiceways, and water gates that kids can manipulate. A new Natural Science area includes an Animal Outpost where kids can observe and learn about live animals in habitat. There's also an expanded greenhouse which buzzes with activity as urban kids make contact with green growing things, and discover plants that have exploding seeds and weeds that can grow twelve feet a year.

The Central Park Carousel

Address: Mid-Central Park at 64th Street
Phone: 879-0244 • Ideal Age Group: 2 to 7
Admission: $1 per person

The facial expression must be genetically encoded because every parent has mastered it—mouth agape, eyes buggy, head tilting slightly backward with an abrupt intake of breath. It's the "carousel face"— the one you use to greet your three-year-old as he or she comes around for the tenth time on the Central Park Carousel. I love that look, kids love that look, and everyone loves this classic, turn-of-the-century merry-go-round. Built in 1903 by the eminent woodcarvers, Stein and Goldstein, it features 58 hand-carved horses, colorful chariots and plump cherubs. The four-minute ride includes the traditional piped-in organ music—you just add the over-the-top facial reactions. A New York childhood is not complete without ten to twenty visits to this carousel annually. Make a morning of it with a visit to the Tisch Children's Zoo (Fifth Avenue at 65th Street/861-6030) and then head home for naptime.

Chinatown Ice Cream Factory

Address: 65 Bayard Street bet. Mott and Elizabeth Streets
Phone: 608-4170 • Ideal Age Group: 2 to 12
Admission: $2.00 per scoop

I f every child's favorite food is pizza, then the favorite dessert has to be ice cream. And the freshest, creamiest, most irresistible ice cream in New York is found right here in this little Chinatown shop. The two Seid Brothers make all thirty-eight flavors on premises from natural ingredients. The Asian specialties—like ginger, litchi, mango, green tea, taro, and red bean—are buttery and exotic. But on a recent visit, I gorged on a double scoop of almond cookie and banana—the most intensely flavored ice creams I've ever tasted. Philip Seid tells me the current favorites among aficionados are Oreo cookie, coconut fudge, and pineapple. Philip's favorite is pistachio (although he looks like a chocolate chip man to me). If you've walked halfway down Mott Street and realized your kids couldn't possibly live without a frozen dessert fix for another week, ask Philip to pack a take-home quart to the brim.

Chuck E. Cheese

**Address: 221 Bergen Mall off Route 4 East, Paramus,
New Jersey
Phone: 201-587-1353 • Ideal Age Group: 2 to 8
Admission: Parties start at $10.99 per child
Web site: www.chuckecheese.com**

Ask parents in Northern New Jersey to name a perennially popular birthday party spot and they'll tell you Chuck E. Cheese. The only reason this huge pizza-and-play franchise (300 locations in the United States) has never invaded the city is that they need thousands of square feet to do what they do; namely, create a decent pizza joint in a child-friendly, arcade-like atmosphere. Chuck E. himself is a playful mouse on steroids, with big buckteeth and a blue-and-red beanie. The illustrious rodent makes an appearance on the half-hour to the approving screams of every pint-sized pizza eater in the place. But the most startling attraction here is the SkyTube, a maze of multicolored tunnels suspended from the ceiling, which you could easily mistake for a ventilation system except for the clusters of kids climbing joyfully through it. Get ready for a strange experience—eating a slice of pizza with toddlers dangling over your head.

Dana Discovery Center

Address: 110th Street near Fifth Avenue
Phone: 860-1370 • Ideal Age Group: 4 to 12
Admission: $5 adults/$1 children

J ust think of it, you and the kids sitting on the shaded bank of a quiet lake, bamboo fishing poles dangling over the water, large-mouth bass flirting with your bait. Colorado, right? Vermont? No, Manhattan. Don't believe me? Then pack a picnic lunch and head to the northernmost end of Central Park. That's where landscape architect Laura Starr joined the Central Park Conservancy to transform the Harlem Meer (an eleven-acre lake) from a debris-filled swamp into a stunning nature area with wetlands, a sandy beach, and a restored brick boathouse. The boathouse is the center of activities for kids year-round, used for environmental education, arts-and-crafts workshops, hands-on science projects and . . . fishing! The lake is stocked with more than 50,000 bass, catfish, shiners, and bluegills for kids to catch and release. The poles, the bait, and all the enriching kid's programs here are free.

Frozen Ropes

Address: 202 W. 74th Street bet. Broadway and Amsterdam
Phone: 362-0344 • Ideal Age Group: 8 to 12
Admission: $40 for half hour up to 5 kids; $75 for one hour
Web site: www.frozenropesnyc.com

In baseball vernacular a "frozen rope" is a sharply hit line drive. But for any future Mike Piazza's or Derek Jeter's in your family, this particular Frozen Ropes hits a home run. Created in the basement of an old bank building, this high-tech baseball training center for kids and adults offers baseball and softball enthusiasts a year-round facility to practice the fine art of hitting, pitching, base running, and fielding. Professional instruction is available, and Frozen Ropes throws an excellent birthday party, too, that can include favors like stadium cups, batting helmets, and personalized baseball bats. But I like the idea of simply taking two of your favorite sluggers down to the cages (they've got four batting cages with state-of-the-art pitching machines) and letting them hit up to 600 balls in the span of an hour. Frozen Ropes isn't cheap, but your kids will be talking about the way they connected with that 70-mph fastball for weeks.

Lazer Park

**Address: 163 West 46th Street bet. Broadway and 6th
Avenue • Phone: 398-3060 • Ideal Age Group: 7 to 12
Admission: $8.95 for single mission of Lazer Tag or
Battletech • Web site: ww.lazerpark.com**

It's a good thing the phaser guns were less than lethal,
because my twin nephews and a half-dozen other hi-tech
fighters on the opposing team pulverized me repeatedly during a recent mission of Lazer Tag. This fast-paced virtual reality game is played New York-style in a 5,000-square-foot
underground arena at action-packed Lazer Park near Times
Square. You strap on computerized flak jackets, shoulder your
light phaser, and dart through a maze of orange and green pil-
lars that look like giant pinball obstacles. With fog swirling at
your feet, and high-decibel music fueling your adrenaline
rush, your senses are on full alert. Lazer Park is also loaded
with the latest interactive arcade and redemption prize games
(at least 70 of them), but it's the thrill of hunting down other
warriors intent on nailing you with their infrared beams that
keeps kids and adults coming back for more.

Lefferts Homestead

Address: Flatbush Avenue, Prospect Park, Brooklyn
Phone: 718-789-2822 • Ideal Age Group: 6 to 12
Admission: Free
Web site: www.prospectpark.org

In a city built predominantly of steel, concrete, and chrome it's completely incongruous to see an old wooden farmhouse. The clapboard Lefferts Homestead was built a year after America declared its independence (1777), and it vibrates with Colonial history. Call for a complete listing of educational and entertaining activities specifically designed for children, most having a Colonial theme—creating old-fashioned toys and puppets, art projects using natural materials, or crafting holiday ornaments using eighteenth-century techniques. The Dutch Colonial homestead is also located just steps from the renovated Prospect Park Wildlife Center, built to perfect child proportions and inhabited by the kind of pettable animals kids love. And before you go, make it a triple play by finishing the day not far away on the fabulously restored Prospect Park Carousel.

New York Firefighter's Friend

Address: 263 Lafayette Street bet. Prince and Spring Streets
Phone: 226-3142 • Ideal Age Group: 3 to 8
Admission: $5 adults/$1 children

If a visit to your neighborhood firehouse has ignited your child's interest in owning something, anything, NYFDish, your best bet is this SoHo specialty shop. Located a couple blocks from the Fire Department's medical center, your kids are likely to bump into a member of New York's Bravest shopping for his or her own fire-theme gifts. For adults they've got new and recycled firemen's coats, but it's the kids' gear that's really hot (sorry). Store owner Nate Freedman carries plenty for fireman wannabes, including black plastic helmets, fire bears, firefighter pajamas, and, of course, black-and-yellow firefighter raincoats that look regulation issue. If you like the traditional T-shirt with FDNY on the front, and KEEP BACK 200 FT. on the flip side, you can also pick them up here in navy, red, or gray, sized for the whole family.

The New York Fire Museum

Address: 278 Spring Street bet. Hudson and Varick Streets
Phone: 691-1303 • Ideal Age Group: 2 to 8
Admission: $4 adults/$1 children (suggested)

Die-hard junior firefighters love this over-stuffed museum. And after September 11, 2001, this tribute to New York's firefighting history has taken on new significance. Situated in a pristine former firehouse, this turn-of-the-century, three-story building is filled with gooseneck hand pumpers, Colonial leather fire buckets, torchlights, axes, alarm boxes, hose nozzles, and a slightly macabre, stuffed firehouse dog that was a favorite of his engine company in the 1940s. You should also know that your neighborhood firehouse is often very kid-friendly. If the firefighters aren't racing off to douse a blaze, and you don't stay too long, you can usually drop by for a fantasy tour. Inside are the rolling red monsters with awesome tires the height of second-graders and water hoses as thick as boa constrictors. And you know why most of the firefighters you'll see leave their shoes untied or wear slip-on shoes? So they can kick them off fast when the alarm sounds and jump into a pair of those big boots lined up against the walls!

New York City Police Museum

Address: 100 Old Slip
Phone: 480-3100 • Ideal AgeGroup: 6 to 12
Admission: $5 adults/$2 children (suggested)/
under 6 yrs. free
Web site: www.nycpolicemuseum.org

To kids, cops are cool. And at this downtown NYPD museum, your children can rub holsters with real police officers. They can also view a wild collection of lethal-looking police weapons and weird bad guy stuff. Some of the memorabilia is commonplace (communications' gear, police shields, whistles), but most of it is sensational—like the counterfeit money with brilliantly copied fives and twenties (I defy you to pick the fakes). There's also a case full of gangster "rub out" paraphernalia—sawed-off shotguns, ice picks, cement blackjacks, brass knuckles, even Al Capone's confiscated tommy gun. I was mesmerized by a bullet display from infamous shootings (gruesome but gripping), a big mug shot camera, and a perfectly restored 1972 Plymouth Fury radio car. If your kids want to take home a T-shirt with an authentic police insignia, visit the Police Museum Gift Shop on the premises.

TRL at MTV

Address: Times Square, 1515 Broadway at 43rd Street
Ideal Age Group: 12 and up • Admission: Free
Web site: www.mtv.com/onair/trl

I'm including this location in a book for children under twelve for one simple reason—your kids are going to be teenagers sooner than you think. Really. And when they do, they will beg you to take them to a taping of *TRL* (Total Request Live), the still insanely popular MTV program. The show's core audience is 16 to 24-year-olds, but the teeming masses of screaming kids who line up behind police sawhorses to watch 3:30 P.M. tapings of the pop-video TV show look like they start at age ten. When likable host, Carson Daly, turns to acknowledge the crowd from the big windows of MTV's visible second-floor studio, the street absolutely erupts. There are actually only 80 audience seats available, so few in the stand-by crowd ever get in, but the scene outside rocks. If you're 15, and you've done the *TRL* thing, you're cool. Enough said.

Wollman Rink

Address: Central Park at 63rd Street
Phone: 439-6900 • Ideal Age Group: 5 to 12
Admission: $8 adult, $5 children, $4 skate rental
(October through April)
Web site: www.wollmanskatingrink.com

The Sky Rink and Roller Blading venues at Chelsea Piers (see page 26) are exceptional, the Rockefeller Center Rink is the stuff of legend, but if you want an unforgettable New York experience, you've got to take the kids ice skating in Central Park. The best place to do that is at the Wollman Rink where there's lots of open sky overhead, trees all around, and the great hotels of Central Park South casting afternoon shadows over the rolling lawns. This skyline view is so breathtaking even children stop their lazy loops to look up and stare. Even more marvelous on winter evenings, come when the glittering lights of the surrounding buildings add to the fantasy feeling. The rink used to be open for in-line skating during the summer months until someone realized that most folks would rather explore the park's miles of meandering pathways. Now you have to save the Wollman Rink for the heavy sweater days of fall and winter.

About the Author

Allan Ishac is an advertising copywriter and creator of the Telly Award-winning Hard Hat Harry™ video series for children. He is a recipient of the Mayor's Volunteer Superstars Award for his bedtime story readings at Beth Israel Hospital in Manhattan and is also the author of *New York's 50 Best Places to Find Peace and Quiet.* He lives right here in this giant theme park—New York City.

About the Illustrator

Katherine Schultz is very fond of New York City. She lived here for five years and worked as a senior artist for the Children's Television Workshop. Katherine lives in Philadelphia where she is earning her master's degree in art education from the University of the Arts.